The Everlasting Now

The Everlasting Now

by

George a. Maloney s.j.

Meditations on the mysteries of life and
death as they touch us in our daily choices.

Ave Maria Press - Notre Dame, Indiana 46556

To all the members of the John XXIII Center for Eastern Christian Studies, those of the past and those of the present who have labored to bring Eastern Christianity to the West.

Acknowledgments:

Sincere thanks to Mrs. Rita Ruggiero for typing this manuscript; to Andrea Federoff, and to Sister Joseph Agnes, S.C.H., for their careful reading and correcting of the manuscript and for the other suggestions that proved most helpful. A special thanks to Dominic Berardino for providing special books used in research. Grateful acknowledgment is made to the following publishers: Darton, Longman & Todd, Ltd., and Doubleday & Company, Inc., N.Y., for excerpts from the Jerusalem Bible, copyright 1966 by Darton, Longman & Todd, Ltd., and Doubleday and Company, Inc. All scriptural texts are from this Bible version unless otherwise noted.

Imprimi Potest: Rev. Vincent M. Cooke, S.J.
                 Provincial of the New York Province
                 September 1, 1979

International Standard Book Number: 0-87793-200-X (Cloth)
                                               0-87793-201-8 (Paperback)

Library of Congress Catalog Card Number: 79-57550

Printed and bound in the United States of America.

Contents

Introduction

The United States and Sweden have the highest annual suicide rate in the world. In America the phenomenon is found chiefly among college students. Such violent deaths by suicide are a tragic confession that many of us have found no meaning in human existence.

Jean-Paul Sartre is the spokesman for a generation of persons who find no such meaning. He writes in *Nausea:* "I was just thinking, that here we sit, all of us, eating and drinking to preserve our precious existence and really there is nothing, nothing, absolutely no reason for existing."[1]

The reality of death is all around, laughing at us with its mocking assurance that it will eventually swallow us into a dark pit of nonbeing. So we spend most of our active lives frantically trying to avoid its finality and certainty. Although we know all humans eventually die, we naively hold out a hope that such a universal law will refuse to be operative in our case.

We easily find ways to refuse to look at death. We seek to amass money, to travel to new places. We search always for new peak experiences so as never to be bored by monotony. Movies, sports, our own creative work can give us temporary relief from the gnawing question: After death, then what?

Sex has become an obsesssion for our modern society. Is there not a relationship between this obsession and a seeking to avoid death? Dr. Rollo May writes:

> Death is the symbol of ultimate impotence and finiteness, and anxiety arising from this inescapable experience calls forth the struggle to make ourselves infinite by way of sex. . . . Repression of death equals obsession with sex. Sex is the easiest way to prove our vitality, to demonstrate we are still "young," attractive and virile, to prove we are not dead yet. [2]

Thus, pathetically, modern man refuses to accept his creatureliness, the fact that he is not really God. By playing roles and posturing he tells his false ego that he is okay! One author, however, insists that we must live as though we are shipwrecked. "All the rest is rhetoric, posturing, farce. He, who does not really feel himself lost, is without remission; that is to say, he never finds himself, never comes up against his own reality."[3]

Search for Meaningfulness

A search for meaning, then, is the real reason why our generation is so worried about death, since death above all puts an end to our created worlds of meaningfulness. Curiously, though we shun thoughts about our personal death, we have a certain fascination with death in general. In the past decade, for example, death has been the subject of a great many books. One writer claims that the subject is rivaling pornography in its appeal for the public's interest. Most of these books deal in a popular way with the psychic phenomena that have been reported either by those attending the deaths of the critically ill or by those who report what they themselves experienced as they "clinically" died and returned to life. Such findings have been collected by psychologists and parapsychologists and published with the conclusion that something of all of us survives in a life after death: therefore, death cannot be *too* bad!

The Christian Vision

Such modern preoccupation with death should make us confront death before our final death. But the current treatment is not the way to do it. This book takes a different approach. It is aimed at Christians who have received a faith vision through God's revelation. This vision tells them that life is a gift from God that is to be developed into meaningfulness, as a seed matures into full fruition, by their free choices to live not for themselves but for God and neighbor. Christians believe that God has revealed to them how to live this present life so that death will not be victorious but will be the passageway into eternal life.

This revelation, found in Holy Scripture and the teachings of the church, presents human existence as an ongoing growth process. Each part in the process, namely, our present life on earth, our dying and our life after death, is to be integrated into the total process of a person stretching out to attain human maturity.

Yet, the majority of Christians do not see their lives as a growth process. What God has revealed to them about the meaning of their earthly existence, about death, about heaven, hell, purgatory, the Mystical Body of Christ, the church, and the resurrection, has not become a living reality for most of them. We think that we really understand the message of Jesus when we accept as literally true the Jewish apocalyptic imagery that he and the Old and New Testament writers used to describe life after death. We think that we can conveniently handle the problem of what awaits us after death by placing such realities about that future life into neat mental boxes that then have very little impact upon our daily choices.

By using our time and space categories to express what Jesus meant to be a total experience in the *kairos* of *now* salvation, we have been able to tuck away safely into the far future the problems of death and what awaits us after death.

The message of Jesus about death, the kingdom of God, final judgment or hell, is an urgent message, a call to begin to live a human life *now,* one that is rooted in death-resurrection, death to self-centeredness and a rising to greater union with God and the whole world through authentic self-sacrificing love.

Death and true life in Christ are all around us. We must make choices at every moment because heaven, hell and purgatory are also being fashioned now by our choices. Our personal judgment and the general judgment are dependent upon this day's choices. We cannot afford to objectify as static entities what Christ has taught us about life after death, because in so doing we all too easily lose his true message as we remove those realities from our present existence.

This book offers a challenge to the Christian reader to reflect prayerfully about the mystery of life and death as these touch him or her *now.* I have attempted to present what the church traditionally has taught in its interpretation of Holy Scripture and in its teaching magisterium about death, life immediately after death, purgatory (or the needed healing therapy), the communion of saints, hell, heaven and the resurrection of the dead.

A Prayerful Reflection

But I would hope to do more. I would hope to lead the average Christian into a dynamic vision of a growth process that would shake up the habitual, static view of such realities concerning life after death and replace this with a process theology of life after death. I would like to involve the reader in a prayerful consideration of the interrelationships of these traditional teachings so that these truths may become living realities, affecting daily Christian living now.

It is an invitation to reflect and to shape new attitudes about the life after death that go beyond the catechism of mere concepts and can influence powerfully the way we presently live. It is a presentation of a Christian perspective, using insights from modern process theologians and the early Eastern Fathers, that will, it is hoped, elicit from the reader a "real" and not merely a "notional" assent to the truths about life after death.

Finally, this book touches the subject of prayer insofar as such self-involving reflections needed to read this book with profit are to be done in a prayerful attitude. It involves the ability of the reader to enter into the mystery, as deeper prayer also requires, of moving beyond our own control over God, our own lives and the lives of others by the cliches we have constructed about life after death, in order to enter into the darkness of facing the terrifying possibility of death and judgment *now*.

Ultimately, death is more than the physical death that surely awaits all of us. It becomes a terrifying experience in our every thought, word or act of selfishness that separates us from God. And true life, as we discover in prayer, becomes the love that we show to God and to each human person met along life's circuitous paths.

The Everlasting Now is what Jesus Christ taught and lived. It is what he holds out for us Christians in our search for ultimate meaningfulness.

George A. Maloney, S.J.

August 15, 1979
Feast of the Assumption of Mary into Heaven

Chapter One
Death Is Growth

At a recent college commencement ceremony, Dr. Elisabeth Kubler-Ross, renowned authority on the psychology of death and dying, summed up her message about death with this simple statement: "At the end of life the only thing that really counts is whether you have had the courage to live."

The courage to live. . . . Perhaps that is why most of us fear not only the thought of death, but also the moment of our dying. We think we have time to accomplish our plans for living more fully and death is the enemy that will thwart them. Don Juan tells Castaneda in *Journey to Ixtlan*:

> You're wrong again. You can do better. There is one simple thing wrong with you—you think you have plenty of time. . . . You don't have time.
>
> My friend, that is the misfortune of human beings. None of us has sufficient time, and your continuity has no meaning in this awesome, mysterious world.[1]

The reality is that death is a terrifying upheaval in our human way. It is a fearful sundering of the only existence we have known up to that moment. It is the most "un-natural" act that we have to undergo in this life. Thus psychologically we learn ways not to think of death or ways of denying that it will ever happen to us. In such ways we can suppress our fears and anxieties.

Western culture helps us in this death-denying pro-cess. Through our affluence and technology we have fashioned a cult of the comfortable. Who dare think of death or speak of that awful possibility when there is so much to live for! Arnold Toynbee, the British historian, writes:

> Death is "un-American"; for, if the fact of death were once admitted to be a reality even in the United States, then it would also have to be admitted that the United States is not the earthly paradise that it is deemed to be (and this is one of the crucial articles of faith in "the American way of life"). Present-day Americans, and other present-day Westerners too in their degree, tend to say, instead of "die," "pass on" or "pass away." [2]

Yet death is all around us. We experience the con-stant process of dissolution in youthful growing pains as well as in middle age and in retirement. As we grow older, our parents, relatives and friends begin to die. Violence and death, so vividly portrayed in the mass media, should become a constant reminder that we too will die. But because it is portrayed as dehumanized and impersonal, we block it out of our consciousness. At least the realization of my personal death is easily dimmed in the light of so many impersonalized deaths.

Reactions to Death

For those who do not allow a faith vision to lead them, one reaction can be that of hedonism: Take all the pleasures you can seize in a given moment (Horace's *carpe diem* or "grasp the day") for you cannot be sure of the next day. The author of the Book of Wisdom places the following words in the mouths of worldlings who see the shortness of earthly life and how death puts an end to all the good things of this life:

> Come, then, let us enjoy what good things there
> are,
> use this creation with the zest of youth;
> take our fill of the dearest wines and perfumes,
> let not one flower of springtime pass us by,
> before they wither crown ourselves with roses.
> Let none of us forego his part in our orgy,
> let us leave the signs of our revelry everywhere,
> this is our portion, this the lot assigned us (Wis
> 2:6-9).

Another reaction to death is extreme pessimism and fatalism. In the fifth century B.C. the Greek poet Sophocles stated that there is "no exit" from a meaningless life. "It is best of all never to have been born and second best—second by far—if one has made his appearance in this world, to go back again, as quickly as may be, thither whence he has come."[3]

The Latin poet Lucretius also laments man's lot ever to have been born, only to suffer in this life and then to pass into annihilation. "Death, then, is null for us—null and irrelevant—in virtue of the conclusion that the spirit of man is mortal."[4]

Atheists or agnostics hope, even though death will annihilate them, that they may live on through their contributions bequeathed to their children or to mankind in the generations to come. The belief, at times, can raise persons to a high level of altruism and unselfishness.

Hinduism and Buddhism teach a pessimism or fatalism in regard to the present life: It is good only to allow an individual to perform his *karma* (the purifications needed to rise from the defects of former lives to a new cycle of reincarnation) until through successive deaths the individual may reach *nirvana.*

Such pessimism toward the value of the individual bears a resemblance to the pessimism of suicide. Here death is regarded as a lesser evil than one's present form of existence.

Of these views, those that lead to despair view man as merely a biological animal that dies and is extinguished. The lack of faith precludes any sense of mystery in death. Others, who hold out a cyclic series of reincarnations until the individual loses his personal identity and becomes immersed in the Ocean of Absolute Being, place all reality in spirit. This leads to the complete rejection of the historical human community.

A Faulty Christian View

Being a Christian does not automatically insure a healthy attitude toward death. Neoplatonic and Gnostic principles have often been the philosophical backdrop used by Christian thinkers such as St. Augustine, Martin Luther, John Calvin and the Jansenists, to articulate a popular Christian view of death. Through an exaggerated distrust of the material world, such thinkers see death as a liberator from this "vale of tears." A modern author describes well such idealists:

> The classic expression of this view appeared in Greek philosophy in the writings of Plato, entered Christian thought in the second and third centuries, found a full-blown exposition in the writings of Augustine, and has been the general mood of Reformed theology from Calvin to the present day. Life is seen as a temporary sojourn from which only death leads to real life. The world is evil, and

therefore life in it is essentially evil as well. Death comes to release us, to deliver our souls from the bodies that constrain them. The idealist sees death as the great liberator, coming to free in man that which is truly human— the soul or spirit—while the body is destroyed.[5]

In such a view the human person is conceived of as essentially an immortal soul. Death is the violent separation of the soul from the body, which is put in a coffin and is to be rejoined to the soul on a far-distant resurrection day. And immediately upon death the soul stands before the all-knowing God who judges its life. We are given a reward of heaven or hell, or are assigned to an intermediate stage called purgatory. In heaven or hell, our state of bliss or punishment is fixed, determined by God's justice. No matter how omnipotent and infinite his love for us is, it cannot coerce us to return our love because of the demands of human freedom and God's own justice. Justice demands no mercy beyond the conditions laid down by God in the beginning.

*   *   *   *   *

We could pause to reflect on what our habitual attitude is toward death. What concept of death is operating when you attend a wake of a funeral? Do you not believe that the body lying in the coffin is the only bodily remains of your relative or friend? In your view, has not the soul of the deceased departed from this shell, the body, and now gone to a place called heaven, hell or purgatory? Does not God judge that person at the very instant the soul departs the body and according to his or her good or bad deeds performed while on earth? Have you not always been taught that the soul is by its nature immortal, therefore it is the body that dies?

I believe we can safely say that most Christians have

inherited such a notion of death. It is based on a Platonic view that splits the human person into two parts—body and soul. The body dies, the soul is immortal. By placing immortality in the soul as a natural attribute, such a Christian view is unable to grasp the full impact of death and almost totally rejects a holistic and biblical view of the total person as a relationship of body and soul that develops both in this life and in the next. Let us try to build a different view of death, not as much as a separation of body and soul, but as a growth process. This will then aid us in understanding how to live as whole persons.

Chapter Two
Toward a Christian Understanding

There is a sense in which we can say that in death there is a separation of the soul from the body. Karl Rahner, in a most creative essay entitled "On the Theology of Death,"[1] claims that the traditional theological description can be legitimately helpful if it is not taken literally as a physical separation of two constitutive parts of a human person. A legitimate use of such a description of separation views man as different from other organic beings. It describes the truth that in death the spiritual life principle assumes a new relationship to the body. Thus there is a *real* severance in a biological sense.

It is not only a body that dies, however, but a whole person that undergoes death. Rahner insists on avoiding the image that the soul "leaves" this world and goes up into a spiritual world, losing all relationships with the material world once the body is dead. He writes:

> It should rather be borne in mind that, even in her lifetime, as informing the body, the spiritual soul is an open system toward the world. It might also be remembered with profit that natural philosophy finds it almost impossible to restrict the idea of the human "body" to what is covered by the skin. The

spiritual soul, moreover, through her essential relationship to the body, is basically open to the world in such a manner that she is never a monad without windows, but always in communication with the whole of the world.[2]

A Biblical View of Man

The biblical view of man, Semitic in nature and not Hellenistic, is seen best represented by St. Paul in his writings. Such a human person is composed of a body (*soma* in Greek) that is for all purposes the whole man as a psychophysical unity, a personality turned toward the created world around him; and the *pneuma* or spirit, the total man as viewed in his unique personality through a knowing relationship in love to God. Man relates to the cosmic world through the body, which is made up of the soul or psyche with all the emotions and passions we call irascible and concupiscible as well as the *sarx* or the flesh. But he also relates to the material world through the pneuma or spirit, which is, however, more transcendent in its relationship to God in a conscious self-giving act of love toward God.

In such a biblical view, death is a rather sudden disruption of man's relationship to the material world through the sarx or flesh. It is one of the most dramatic events in man's evolution, allowing man definitively to move into a greater consciousness through a dying to the vegetable and animal life in him. Such a whole person, the biblical *soma*, the body-man, in his personality toward the world, now becomes more open to the whole universe.

These are the expressions of modern theologians, such as Rahner, Paul Chauchard and others[3] who teach that death does not bring about a separation of the biblical body and soul, but it brings an end to our immersion in a lower stage of evolutionary development, namely, the vegetable and animal level. Thus the human person in death moves higher to where he or she now relates in greater intensity both *outward* toward the cosmic world through an expanding awareness of his or her solidarity with the material world and in greater intensity inward toward God in a greater realization of his or her unique being in relationship to him.

Do such views stimulate us to examine our habitual understanding of death? Have you never felt that, in spite of the many tensions experienced in your earthly life between the body, soul and spirit levels of relationships, you always remained a single person in your consciousness? You usually say, "I ache in my head," or "I feel sad," or "I pray to God." It is the whole person, my total *I-ness* in a particular relationship of body or soul or spirit that undergoes such an experience. The whole person is the subject of consciousness, not a part.

What such thinkers are telling us is that the whole human person undergoes death. But they are also saying that death leads us to a new level of growth. After death we continue as the same persons enjoying the same level of consciousness attained during the earthly existence through our body, soul and spirit relationships.

Such a more biblical view of man as a total person facing death brings us to the question of why we have to die at all. Is not death an evolutionary step toward greater cosmic consciousness and therefore toward greater responsibility to aid in the full and final consummation of the universe? Will not man with the aid of science eventually do away with death?

The Wages of Sin Are Death

From scripture and the constant teaching of the church death is seen as a result of sin. In original justice, the way God had intended mankind to live in relationship to himself and the rest of created nature, grace brought man into a deep communion with God. The sin of man's independence outside of a loving obedience to God's wishes broke this union radically. This break is dramatically described in the words from the Book of Genesis: "So Yahweh God expelled him from the garden of Eden" (Gn 3:23). Man, before he had sinned, therefore, could have lived immune from death or, if he were to die, such a transition into a higher level of conscious evolution would have been likened more to a sleep than the violent upheaval it is now because of sin.

To better understand this teaching let us draw again from the important distinction given by Karl Rahner. Death is something passively suffered. It happens to all of us and even could have happened to the first man had he not sinned. This is the biological aspect that brings a definitive end to our "natural" way of existing through a material body in space and time relationships to the rest of the material world around us. Through such natural relationships as a bodied being, man become a *person* as he freely chooses to make of himself *himself*, that unique person capable of freely giving himself in love to God and neighbor.

It is this personal element that varies for each individual as he or she faces death. What happens to you on the biological level is commonly shared with all human beings. You can do very little as you "suffer" death to happen to you. But death as "act" is a human being confronting death and freely ordering this act toward an ultimate end. Rahner describes this important insight that can give us true understanding of death as caused by sin:

> But how he dies his death and how he understands it, depends on the decision of his freedom. Here he does not carry

something imposed on him, but what he chooses himself. That is to say: in the deed of the dying existence, man is necessarily free in his attitude toward death. Although he has to die, he is asked how he wishes to do it. For, existence conscious of itself must unavoidably see the end. It sees this end all through life, perhaps dimly and not explicitly. It may happen that it will purposely avoid looking at it, or it will simply overlook it (but still will realize it all the same). Inasmuch as man freely takes upon himself this existence tending toward the end, he also freely accepts the movement toward the end.[4]

We can understand revelation's teaching about the first man's possibility of reaching fulfillment without a death due to sin if we can see man taking his life in hand and freely affirming himself in total self-surrendering love to God. He would have been freed of our experience of death as the passive suffering of a violent upheaval caused by an outside force. Death for man before the fall would have been an active movement in grace to the deepest oneness with God and an accompanying cosmic consciousness of his oneness with the entire, created world.

It is this same act of shaping your being from the depths of your personhood that can still be part of death as we know it, after sin. It should be this free act, not only on your deathbed but throughout your whole life, that imparts to your Christian life and death a share in Christ's eternal, risen life that conquers sin and death (Rom 8:2).

And, although Jesus Christ conquered sin and death and hence you can scorn death as an effect of sin since it no longer has a sting or victory over you (1 Cor 15:55), still death does exhibit for all of us the aspect of a punishment for sin. Death, as you experience it in this order of salvation, should not exist. Even if you are in the grace of Christ, there is a fear that attacks the faith, hope and love poured into your hearts by the Spirit of Jesus.

Who can say that, even rooted strongly in Christlike virtues, he or she cannot in the face of death lose hope in God's mercy? Can you not freely in that ultimate act of self-determination hesitate, doubt, rely on your own strength and reasoning? There is a darkness in death that all of us, saints and sinners and those in between, must undergo that can be conceived of as a part of the "wages of sin" (Rom 6:23).

So in a real way you can accept the scriptural and doctrinal teaching as proposed by the church's magisterium down through the centuries that there are definitely elements in death as we now must experience it that are the result of sin, both of the first man as well as of society and of your own sinful actions. In death you must still opt freely to let God be total Lord of your lives. You reach in death the climax of a lifetime of choosing for God or for yourself.

Dr. Kubler-Ross in her book *On Death and Dying*[5] brings together five stages that dying persons usually pass through before they can accept the "natural" aspects of death.

These are: 1. The dying person experiences an initial stage of shock and denial. 2. He then shows anger and resentment toward loved ones, nurses, doctors and visitors. 3. Then he begins to bargain and sets up conditions to be fulfilled before he is ready to die. 4. The person becomes depressed. 5. Then he accepts the fact of imminent death.

At any stage an individual may stop and go no farther, or death may prevent the movement toward full acceptance. Life is made up of a series of death situations in which we can be angry and resentful toward God because of what we think he is causing to happen to us against our own wills and desires. We can even yield to deep periods of depression and despair. All of these attitudes, like those we may have toward our final death, indicate a need of inner healing by an ever-increasing childlike faith, hope and love. Our degree of complete loving abandonment to God's providential care in each of life's "death" situations will be an indication of how we shall accept our final death.

Death Is So Sweet!

Modern techniques and mechanical apparatuses, which often resuscitate people who have "died" biologically, pose another problem in facing death that is the opposite of the temptation to despair. That is the problem of an overly optimistic view. Dr. Kubler-Ross in her books[6] and her many public lectures throughout the country, along with Dr. R.A. Moody and his interviews with those who have reportedly come back from the dead,[7] has done much to create an optimism in regard to death. This optimism might lessen the pangs of sin and the reality of death, not only as a punishment but also as the most important moment of full, personal decision as a human being strives in the throes of death to reach total self-realization.

Dr. Karlis Osis and Dr. Erlendur Haraldsson, working under the auspices of The American Society for Psychical Research have done one of the most scientific studies on afterlife experiences in researching over 1000 cases both in America and India. They did most of their interviews with doctors and nurses who recorded their experiences in working at the side of dying patients. With such trained medical personnel describing what they witnessed, Dr. Osis and Dr. Haraldsson offer a description of what was commonly recorded and experienced by more than 1000 patients on the point of dying. They

have a modern Lazarus give this advice to us who have
not yet died:

> When your heart stops and the hour of death
> comes, you will not break up and disintegrate
> like ice in the rapids of a river. Instead, it will
> be like diving into a new kind of reality. You
> will feel well and and be happy in a very
> special way — "the peace which passeth all
> understanding." The weariness, the pain,
> and the sadness all will be left with the sheets
> on the hospital bed. You will "light up from
> within," and then you will see someone
> warm and caring waiting to receive you. If
> your own close relatives are suitable for the
> task—and you for them—one will "pop in" as
> lifelike and loving as when you last saw him.
> But there will be a strange air of serenity
> around him. If the situation calls for profes-
> sional help, a religious figure will come in
> brilliant light. Whoever they are, the visitors
> will "turn you on." Something mild but
> powerful will envelop you. It will feel like the
> best moments of your life . . . you might have
> to grope for words—*sacred, light, love.* No,
> none will really do, but you will feel it in the
> core of your being. . . . The heartrending
> anguish of weeping relatives will appear to be
> childish and beside the point. Your own
> grand concerns—the unfulfilled dreams of
> the future, duties to loved ones, work,
> everything you ever looked foward to—will
> become small and unimportant, fading like
> dried flowers. With a sudden wave of joy,
> you will be ready to go.[8]

Such descriptions deal with the psychic experiences
of dying persons. If you are to accept them as the manner
in which all of us will die, there is a danger of naive op-

timism that death is sweet and a very logical step to a fuller life. Christians should truly believe that death does open us up to the fuller life that Jesus Christ promised. The accent, however, must not be placed primarily on how you will *feel* when you die, but on whether you will bring a lifetime of loving relationships to bear on that ultimate moment of total and free surrender in the deepest faith, hope and love.

If people believe that, regardless of how they have lived on this earth, their death will be sweet, ushering them into a more beautiful life than this one ever could be, I am afraid life and death as a continuous process will be ignored by them. We truly will die as we have lived. The continuity must not be ignored. Death, therefore, positively can help you to clarify the purpose and style of life you are to live in order that death may open you up to a full, personal, free, loving surrender of yourself to God.

The Death of Jesus

You, as a Christian, can understand the awesome mystery of death by prayerfully considering the death of Jesus. His death was his long-awaited hour, the baptism he had to receive and great was his distress till it was over (Lk 12:50). His death was a point in time and it took place on a hill outside Jerusalem. But his death was his entire life as he strove to die to his own self-interests and to live in loving surrender to his heavenly Father.

Each moment of Jesus' earthly life was a preparation for his final death. Each choice was made in ever-growing freedom to place his life, every thought, word and deed, under the good pleasure of his Father. He was in all things like us, save sin (Heb 4:15), for no one could convict him of sin (Jn 8:26). There was no injustice in him (Jn 7:18) because he always did what pleased his heavenly Father (Jn 8:29).

The human growth as a person in the life of Jesus consisted in the existential struggle for unity between his consciousness and the various levels of his inner unconsciousness. As Jesus learned to live in greater interiority by centering all his thoughts, words and actions upon the indwelling Father, he learned to let go of the control he exercised over his own human existence. The temptations that he endured in the desert and those in the agony of Gethsemane and on the cross show us something of Jesus entering into the inner combat, an inner dying process, to win the gift of freedom through a new victory of loving, self-abandonment to his Father. Like Adam and all of us, at the core of the temptations that Jesus underwent was the struggle between a state of independence away from submission to his Father and that of free surrender in loving obedience to the Father's will.

Freedom for Jesus as for you is God's gift through the Spirit of love, but it is won by a great struggle wherein the isolated self surrenders to the true self in love, freely given. Without conflict, even in the development of Jesus' human freedom, there could be no growth in freedom, in love and in his full personhood.

Our frequent contemplation of Jesus on the cross, through the aid of plastic crucifixes or by details offered us by a baroque type of pious preacher or spiritual writer, has dimmed for most of us the awful starkness of the scene of his death on Calvary. On Calvary you can discover through the power of the Spirit in prayerful contemplation what death meant to Jesus. But you can at the same time discover the meaning of his life and yours also.

If we fail to contemplate the mystery of God's love revealed for us in Jesus' death unto the last drop of blood, we will resort to some legalistic "satisfaction" theory of atonement. Man in such a theory sinned and contracted a huge debt that he could never pay back. But Jesus Christ as God could offer to his Father on our behalf a payment that canceled the debt. As man, he was able to do this by dying. Rahner shows the inadequacies of such a theory.[9]

The Kenosis of Jesus

Jesus heals and saves you, not in a static moment on the cross. But he affects your redemption throughout his whole existential life of himself to the Father out of love for you when he died on the cross. This saving process admits of great growth on your part as you contemplate this mystery of your redemption in prayer through the illumination of the Holy Spirit. You learn with St. Paul (Gal 2:20) that he died for you personally.

Jesus suffered not as a helpless victim who was passively put to death. His life was not taken from him but he freely gave his life back to the Father in total self-giving with the maximum freedom which measured the purity of his love for the Father. Throughout his whole life Jesus freely chose, when there were possibilities, to descend into the heart of man who was lost. When scripture says that he descended into hell, and that God was "freeing him from the pangs of Hades" (Acts 2:24), it means more than what 1 Peter 3:18 implies, namely, that he went to Hades to preach to the "spirits in prison."[10] He chose to descend into the suffering, dying heart of humanity. He freely wished to become the poorest of the poor, the loneliest of all abandoned human beings.

As the Prophet Isaiah foretold, he willed to be crushed as a worm beneath the cruel heel of this world that crushes so many other men and women as worms and not human beings. He freely willed, by a human choice, to taste *every* ingredient in the bitter chalice that the world, in which the mystery of evil rules, can press to human lips. By Christ's freely wanting to be so completely associated with humanity and God's created world that was groaning in travail (Rom 8:23), he speaks in that radical oneness with our broken world as the perfect image of the Father who also wants to be radically one in his self-giving to us. Now the heavenly Father has a physical presence in his Word made flesh and "descended into hell," as the Creed professes. It is the Father who is now present and speaking to us in the torn, mangled body of Jesus hanging on the cross, yelling out in the agony of being abandoned by the Father who loved him so much. "See, I have branded you on the palms of my hands" (Is 49:16). The heavenly Father in a marvelous way, through the death of Jesus and his "descent into hell," is able to be God among us, as a suffering, self-emptying God.

Jesus in his service to the world, entering into the very depths of sin and death and utter emptiness of self, was choosing humanly to be like God. How beautifully this is brought out in the following text from the Epistle to the Hebrews:

> During his life on earth, he offered up prayer and entreaty, aloud and in silent tears, to the one who had the power to save him out of death, and he submitted so humbly that his prayer was heard. Although he was Son, he learnt to obey through suffering; but having been made perfect, he became for all who obey him the source of eternal salvation and was acclaimed by God with the title of high priest of the order of Melchizedek (Heb 5:7-10).

In the death of Jesus we find the model for all Christians who are faced with death. "The Father loves me because I lay down my life in order to take it up again. No one takes it from me; I lay it down of my own free will . . ." (Jn 10:17). Jesus reaches his full human potential as he freely surrenders his life to the Father. He suffers the same biological pains as any other human being suffering crucifixion. But he *actively* brings together his whole lifetime of freely surrendering in love to his Father his entire being in every thought and action. Nowhere as on the cross does Jesus enter into the fullness of his humanity in his free gift of self back to the Father. You could say also that nowhere during his lifetime does he so enter into the fullness of his divinity revealed as love poured out.

The Glory of the Cross

The secret of an authentic Christian death lies in the power of the cross. It is a logic and wisdom that go beyond the rational control of human nature. "The language of the cross may be illogical to those who are not on the way to salvation, but those of us who are on the way see it as God's power to save" (1 Cor 1:18). St. Paul tells us of the power and the wisdom of God — "God's own foolishness is wiser than human wisdom and God's weakness is stronger than human strength" (1 Cor 1:25).

Because of man's fall and sin in our members (Rom 7:23), we are forced to live on two planes: nature and spirit. C.S. Lewis in his *Screwtape Letters* describes human beings as amphibians living in two worlds:

> Humans are amphibians—half spirit and half animal. . . . As spirits they belong to the eternal world, but as animals they inhabit time. This means that while their spirit can be directed to an eternal object, their bodies, passions, and imaginations are in continual change, for to be in time means to change.[11]

The cross stands at the junction of our twofold identity, at the parting of the ways between the natural and the spiritual worlds. This stands also at the parting of a Christian's view toward death and that of someone not informed by the wisdom of God, made manifest in Christ Jesus. It is a wisdom that is more than logical, conceptual knowledge derived by man's power alone through his natural sense life. This is a wisdom that is an operative knowledge which has power to change darkness into light, absurdity into ultimate meaningfulness, death into true life.

Your whole Christian life should be put under the cross as Jesus himself insisted: "Unless a wheat grain falls on the ground and dies, it remains only a single grain; but if it dies, it yields a rich harvest" (Jn 12:24). He insisted, against the wisdom of the world, that if anyone wanted to be his disciple and obtain eternal life, he had to begin by a "dying" process. He had to enter into a suffering, but such that would deliver him unto a new life. He had to take the risk of surrendering himself in faith to him by giving up a lower level of self-possession which allowed him to be in dominance, ruling his own life, to accept Christ's offer to move unto a higher level of existence to be guided by his Holy Spirit.

> If anyone wants to be a follower of mine, let him renounce himself and take up his cross and follow me. For anyone who wants to save his life will lose it; but anyone who loses his life for my sake will find it (Mt 16:24-25).

Chapter Three
Christian Suffering — A Dying

Suffering will be the lot of every human being. You can stoically accept it with a fatalistic attitude or as the price of punishment for past sins. But Jesus Christ came to give you a vision of faith and the strength through his indwelling life to "suffer with him that we also may be glorified together" (Rom 8:17). Just as in your final death, so in your sufferings that constitute a form of continual dying, there are passive and active diminishments. These you must actively determine by a free choice to move to a higher transcendence through a self-forgetting, a self-sacrificing love.

As Job found out, suffering will always remain a mystery to man's puny reasoning powers. But the Christian understands through the infusion of the Holy Spirit that there is an inward dimension to his or her suffering and death, that is immortal and incorruptible, that is beyond the ravages of decay and pain. That inward dimension lies in God and the indwelling trinitarian life that unfolds within man's being, giving him power to bring life where there are seemingly only suffering and death.

This inward power is the personalized presence and loving energies of the triune family of God, not merely waiting for man to become divinized, but also for God who is always moving toward man in an act of freely "laying down his life for his friend" (Jn 15:13). God is the "philanthropos," the lover of mankind, who is always moving toward self-emptying in order that man might be filled with a sharing in God's own life.

God wishes to make you participators in his own nature (2 Pt 1:4). God freely "suffers" in order that you might become God by grace. This is the Christian view of divinization (*Theosis*, as the Greek Fathers called it) whereby God, in the much-quoted words of St. Irenaeus, became man in order that man might become God.

You reach your fullness of unique personhood in becoming the true person that God wishes you to be, not by being assimilated into the Absolute Ocean of Being, but by freely opting to die to your false self in order to rise to your self in Christ Jesus.

It is this inward dimension of God's loving presence as mystery that leads you through the cross to resurrection. It is this faith, hope and love exercised in each of life's moments that will allow you to rise above the merely natural. Suffering in your daily life will not be conquered by your human, rational powers. It will be conquered in the seeming emptiness of each dark moment. A mystery that entails suffering and dying cannot belong to the domain of *having* or *conquering*. It is in the realm of *being* and *presence*, of yielding through loving submission and self-surrender to a superior power that is, however, the Supreme in self-giving. In the words of the French philosopher Gabriel Marcel, it is something "of which I cannot dispose in any way: which I cannot possess."[1]

You begin to learn how to die from early childhood. There are biological, psychological and spiritual sufferings that "happen" to you and are necessary if you are to grow more fully on the levels of body, soul and spirit relationships. There are your sufferings — sickness, bunglings, the bunglings of others, the fears and anxieties rising from your own humanness and sinfulness.

There will be suffering on a more active level of working by the sweat of your brow for your daily bread. This will entail much monotony and discipline. It calls for a usual, banal routine that in the ultimate analysis cuts away from your egoism as you learn to transcend the momentarily monotonous into a larger vision of creative labor.

The Suffering of Love

Perhaps the greatest call to suffering and dying comes from what apparently should be the most humanizing and most pleasant: from human love. You grow most as a human being when another person calls you to forget and surrender yourself for that person in true, self-sacrificing love.

Love is always an invitation to suffer, for it means to say "yes" to another. Entailed in this acceptance to love is a "no" to any conflicting selfishness. The more you have learned to let go in the mystery of true human love, the more you will be able to live with the mystery of death. For it will be God's spirit of love that will give you the experience to maintain a healthy tension between death and resurrection. You can live in such situations that normally build up fears and anxieties when you approach them only with "natural" force, and show forth love, peace and joy, the fruit of the Holy Spirit (Gal 5:22).

Related to this growth by dying in human love is the union that you can experience in your personal prayer life as you learn to push your consciousness even into the darkness of the unconscious and there surrender to the healing power of God.

St. John of the Cross describes these dyings as the "night of the senses" and the "night of the spirit." They are the closest experiences we human beings can have of not only "suffering" death but also "doing" our death by freely wanting to enter into this action with a complete abandonment of ourselves to the infinite love and mercy of God and allow him to do with us whatever he wishes. Such experiences are known to the contemplatives in this life who, through long years of living in the desert of their inner poverty, are allowed to enter deeper into darkness through the gifts of faith, hope and love. There they touch the innermost depths of their humanness, of their sinfulness, of a oneness with the whole broken world. It is there that they, like Jesus, learn to "descend into hell."

Allow me to quote from a letter that a contemplative nun wrote me recently in which she described her "descent."

> The realization of what sin lies so deeply rooted within me is at times so profound and clear that truly "death and hell are all about." In July this profound sight of the state of my soul was laid open for the first time. I became so horrified that I cursed the state of my miserable soul and I cursed at God, my Life and Breath. I was near total despair. During the five days which followed, I lived in the depths of hell with every terror. (Do not think I am exaggerating, Father, when I tell you this.) The rebellion to God and other persons reaches at times to great and frightful heights! It seems that I will it with an evil intent, and yet, in mercy I beg that I may not will it. Now I understand what I read in the lives of some saints when they told how they went into hell. The hate, the coldness, the terrible emptiness! From an unknown depth, a hidden, most secret desire arises to call to God for salvation, but, it is impossible. I was wholly unable to call to God.

In this grace I came to a bright, new understanding of myself and of the sin in each of us, our inherent weakness and of the fall of Adam. A most tremendous gift, this! Yet, although I hoped for contrition, hardness and cold gripped me. I prayed for tears, yet this "touch" was also withheld. . . . There are also times when I think that I have gone astray, moving away from my salvation and hope instead of toward him.

. . .In the thickness of this cloud, it appears clear that I bear no love or affection for God or anyone else. At such times, I am unable to ask for help from anyone, unable to call out to the Lord, unable to make an act of love or faith or abandonment. Even though when my oppression is not so heavy, I ask for an increase of love and faith. When it is heavy, I cannot seemingly manage even this interior act, small as it is.

Death Is Conquered

Suffering of any kind can be a death of a sort to your own egoism in order that Jesus Christ can be full Master and Lord in your life. As you die to your self-centeredness and place Christ as the center, you begin to live out your baptism as you experience a new union with the indwelling Lord. St. Paul writes: "Let your thoughts be on heavenly things, not on the things that are on the earth, because you have died, and now the life you have is hidden with Christ in God. But when Christ is revealed—and he is your life—you too will be revealed in all your glory with him" (Col 3:2-4). You perform your greatest witness to the afterlife, not only on your deathbed before your loved ones as you joyfully accept the mystery of death as a gift from God but also in each moment of your life as you proclaim to those around you through your example that there is life eternal even now in the given sufferings of the day.

Your faith in Jesus Christ who has conquered over sin and death should be so great that even as you live, and above all as you finally die, you know with assurance given by the Spirit of the risen Jesus that in the words of the Prophet Isaiah: "The Lord Yahweh will wipe away the tears from every cheek" (Is 25:8). You, as a Christian, should witness to a pragmatic world, which measures reality in terms of present quantitative power or pleasure, that God, through Jesus Christ, has entered into death and has conquered it in Christ's humanity.

That same power of Christ is in you as a Christian, allowing you to overcome corruption and sin, death and meaninglessness. That power brings you into life, that you might have it more abundantly (Jn 10:10). You have put on Christ who lives in you. In all of your weaknesses you become strong because of his strength in you. The words of Hosea become yours as with Christ you can shout to life's daily deaths and finally to death itself, "Where is your plague, Death? Where are your scourges, Sheol?" (Hos 13:14). St. Paul had truly experienced the saving power of Jesus Christ daily, long before he entered into his final death when he wrote:

> When this perishable nature has put on imperishability, and when this mortal nature has put on immortality, then the words of Scripture will come true: Death is swallowed up in victory. Death, where is your sting? Now the sting of death is sin, and sin gets its power from the Law. So let us thank God for giving us the victory through our Lord Jesus Christ (1 Cor 15:54-58).

You, Christian, learn daily to live a constant death to yourself. "I face death every day," St. Paul writes (1 Cor

15:31). By exercising faith, hope and love in the context of each moment lived in Christ and with Christ you can stretch out toward a spiritual maturity that will allow you to be so united to the indwelling Trinity that nothing in life or death can ever separate you from the love of Christ Jesus (Rom 8:38). You as a mature Christian will experience a peace and certitude, not in any reliance on your own good works, not in any magical way of having once and for all been saved, but in the conscious experience that the heavenly Father has placed his power and blessings in you just as Jesus knew that same indwelling power (Jn 13:3).

You begin even now in this pilgrimage on earth, while still in the mortal body, to experience something of immortality, incorruptibility, the unchangeability of God's eternal love for you. In a word, you have entered even now before death has taken you from this mortal existence into a sharing of the resurrection of Jesus Christ. You are a living member of his risen body. By faith you see Jesus' resurrectional presence and his intercessory power as a dynamic force within the material universe. The presence of the risen Jesus sends into your heart the Holy Spirit who imparts to you the very "uncreated energies" of God, making you a child of God. Such energies influence even now your body since you are a whole person meeting the Spirit of Jesus through body, soul and spirit relationships.

> And if the Spirit of him who raised Jesus from the dead is living in you, then he who raised Jesus from the dead will give life to your own mortal bodies through his Spirit living in you (Rom 8:11).

Tied intrinsically to your material body, which is destined to a future redemption through the resurrection, is the whole universe. Christ's glory must be seen in his relationships with the whole material world. Jesus in glory is an active leaven inserted into the mass of creation to raise the whole created world into the fullness destined for it by the Father. And you, who are in Christ, are called by your daily life of living out your baptism and the sacrament and sacrifice of Jesus Christ in the Eucharist to be his reconciler of the whole world to God.

> And for anyone who is in Christ, there is a new creation; the old creation has gone, and now the new one is here. It is all God's work. It was God who reconciled us to himself through Christ and gave us the work of handing on this reconciliation . . . and he has entrusted to us the news that they are reconciled. So we are ambassadors for Christ; it is as though God were appealing through us, and the appeal that we make in Christ's name is: be reconciled to God (2 Cor 5:17-20).

It is the Holy Spirit of the risen Jesus who constantly sheds his divine light upon you to enlighten you to see all things in God's original plan. You are unmoved by opinions or fancies of other worldly-minded men and women. All events are seen in the light of eternity. For such a Christian, the risen Jesus is a continued experience even now. You can truly mock death that received its hold on mankind through sin. Jesus has truly conquered sin and death in you.

> But we believe that having died with Christ we shall return to life with him: Christ, as we know, having been raised from the dead will never die again. Death has no power over him any more. When he died, he died, once for all, to sin, so his life now is life with God; and in that way, you too must consider

yourselves to be dead to sin but alive for God
in Christ Jesus (Rom 6:8-11).

Freedom to Live

Most people are concerned with the wrong questions. They want to know when death will come and
how. They wish to know what their resurrectional bodies
will be like. They are concerned from time to time about
what heaven will be like and usually their ideas are mere
extensions of the space-time existence they know now.
As a Christian, you should not be overly concerned with
such questions but with the great, haunting question:
How can I today, in this moment, be led from fear and
anxiety into being a true child of God, freed from
selfishness and death and the false values of the world
around me and to live in the freedom of the risen people
of God?

Jesus is victor over death and he conquers your
heart so that you may allow him to be Lord in your life.
Freedom is the progressive surrender in love to him so
that in each moment he is Lord. He is the inner force that
allows you to catch this moment of history in all its
brokenness, filth, confining meaninglessness and raise it
to the level of God's *eternal now.* His Spirit brings you into an ever-growing awareness of your true dignity before
the world. In that dignity of being loved infinitely by God
in Christ Jesus, you become progressively more free to
love as he loves you. Freedom, as God gives you this
great gift, is nothing less than the gift of loving yourself
and the entire world as God loves you and with God's
love in you.

Your final death is important, for it is the final opportunity to enter into the darkness of what seems meaningless to your human reasoning and there opt to surrender yourself into the loving hand of your heavenly
Father. Then, in spite of what you may have to suffer in

pain and the temptation to doubt that there is life beyond the end of this earthly road, you can cry out with Jesus a triumphal victory chant: "Father, into your hands I commit my spirit" (Lk 23:46). But you cannot arrive at the final moment of victory over death and a share in the resurrection of Jesus Christ unless you pass through all the moments that bring you to the final one. Death and resurrection no longer become something to accept. They become living realities experienced as you strive to live out the divine life given to you in embryonic form in your first baptism into the Body of Christ. By daily dying to egoism and living for Christ you can share progressively more in his risen life. You can share this vision of hope and joy with all who are heavily burdened with suffering, above all, with those in sin and in the throes of final death.

The authentic test of how much you have truly died in this life and are already risen in Christ must be measured by how much you live for others.

> We have passed out of death and into life,
> and of this we can be sure
> because we love our brothers.
> If you refuse to love, you must remain dead;
> to hate your brother is to be a murderer,
> and murderers, as you know, do not have eternal
>   life in them.
> This has taught us love—
> that he gave up his love for us;
> and we, too, ought to give up our lives for our
>   brothers. . . .
> My children,
> our love is not to be just words or mere talk,
> but something real and active;
> only by this can we be certain
> that we are children of the truth
> and be able to quieten our conscience in his
>   presence (1 Jn 3:14-20).

These chapters have presented death as a growth process. A vision has been presented to you that opposes the understanding which you have held about death as a separation of the immortal soul from the corruptible body. This vision, rooted in Holy Scripture, presents you as a whole person, growing into eternal life by the series of death moments that lead you throughout your entire earthly existence out of the tomb of selfishness into the broad daylight of the freedom of being a child of God.

You live in the infallible truth that Jesus reveals to all of us: "I tell you most solemnly, whoever keeps my word will never see death" (Jn 8:51). His word or commandment is clear: "So this is the commandment that he has given us, that anyone who loves God must also love his brother" (Jn 4:21).

But such a vision cannot be taught. You need prayerfully to reflect on the true meaning of death. God reveals to his children that the true life that he gives us when we love one another is eternal and that no one can ever take it away forever. Thus the death that was revealed as a part of the wages of sin has been conquered and transformed by Jesus Christ into the occasion for claiming eternal life. It is said that you die as you live. It is much truer to say, "You die as you have loved." Then the words of Jesus at the tomb of Lazarus become your daily experience, climaxing in the ultimate experience of death and life through love:

> I am the resurrection.
> If anyone believes in me, even though he
> dies he will live,
> and whoever lives and believes in me
> will never die.
> Do you believe this? (Jn 11:25-26).

Chapter Four
After Death What?

You have just died. Now what? Whether you have a Virgil or a Beatrice to guide you over the threshold, is there an *Inferno* awaiting you or a *Purgatorio* or a *Paradiso?* It is natural that we human beings should inquire as to the future that awaits us after death. Every religion and culture through the ages by means of myths and symbols has sought to give a satisfying answer to this mystery.

And it is wholesome for you to seek an answer to the question: After death, what happens to me? The many modern (and even ancient) recorded experiences of what happened psychologically to persons who seemingly died and came back are just that: a psychological description of a transient experience of a process that never quite makes it over to the "other side" to stay. We are asking: What happens when I pass from death into the other life? Where do I go? What will I be like? Will I be the same person I was in this earthly life? Will others recognize me for who I am? Will I recognize them and will I be able to communicate with them? Will I have a chance in such communication to grow and evolve into someone better (or worse)?

Such questions are not useless ones. We have a built-in, probing curiosity to know not only the next step we are taking in any process of movement, but also the final goal toward which we are journeying. As human beings, we want to know where we are going. We have been given an intellect by God to know a purpose in life and a will freely to choose means to lead us to possess what we know to be the aim of our life. To be traveling and not know the why and the where brings us into a frustration and meaninglessness that eventually leads to some form of irrationality.

Is There a Life?

The most basic question that you need to answer in order to determine how to live now is: Will there be a life after I die? You have been given by God a powerful zest for life, a burning desire to live forever. When your only experience of life is earthly existence, then you want to hold on to this form of life as long as you can. You cannot consciously bear the thought of ceasing to live.

Yet along with this desire for everlasting life, you encounter all around you the certainty of death in numerous forms. Your loved ones, parents, brothers and sisters, friends, neighbors, the famous ones of this world, popes, presidents, movie stars. . . all grow old and die. You discover early in life the dying process within you. You must give up being an infant, a child, an adolescent, a young man or woman in order to become an adult. As soon as you reach maturity in your creative powers, suddenly such powers begin to diminish.

Physical and psychological changes constantly occur within you that should convince you of the reality of death. Although you can learn ways of putting the awful truth out of your mind, you have a certainty that, like your predecessors, you too shall die. You do not have to accept this stark truth on faith. You *know* it for a certain fact!

But is there life after that death? How can you ever know with certainty that there is life and what it will be like? You probe searchingly into the world around you to find some clues to your question. The butterfly emerges from the cocooned chrysalis stage that was formed out of the caterpillar. The snake sheds its skin and still continues to exist. Fruit trees that seemed dead in winter burst into spring blossoms to bring forth new fruit in the fall harvest. So you hope that "this mortal nature must put on immortality" (1 Cor 15:53).

The Light of Reason

Your reason throws its light on the darkness of your uncertainties about a life after death. You can argue philosophically that because you are capable of spiritual operation, you possess faculties that are spiritual and immortal. You can reason yourself toward a "reasonable" belief that, if God made you according to his own image and likeness (Gn 1:26), this would not be a temporal relationship but would continue forever.

In such a likeness to God who is love, you would perhaps expect that such a spiritual power to love would not perish but only continue to develop. How can one who loves another, you ask, do anything but want to continue to grow in greater loving union? Surely God's justice would demand that those who have died before having reached maturity would be given a fair chance to develop and experience loving relationships with God and other human beings in a future life after death.

God's Revelation

No matter what you can marshal together by way of rational reinforcements, you will always have a gnawing doubt as to the certainty of a future life beyond your earthly existence. We can know with moral certitude that some form of life awaits us after death but only on the authority of God who must reveal this knowledge to us. This is a truth that is certain knowledge, given to those of us who open ourselves in transcendent self-presence to God's revealing presence. We accept his revelation by his gift of faith, hope and love, poured into our hearts by the Holy Spirit (Rom 5:5).

God's constant revelation of himself to mankind is that of a loving Father who shares his eternal life with human beings. He is a God who can know no end and he is a God of the living and not of the dead. Against the Sadducees who denied the resurrection and any life after death, Jesus Christ argues from the words of Moses, who declared before the burning bush (Ex 3:4) that the Lord is the God of Abraham, Isaac and Jacob. "Now he is God, not of the dead, but of the living, for to him all men are in fact alive" (Lk 20:38).

For this reason did God create the human race, not to destroy it, but that every man and woman would live and share eternally his divine life (1 Tm 2:16; 1 Jn 2:2; Jn 12:32). "Yes, God loved the world so much that he gave his only Son, so that everyone who believes in him may not be lost but may have eternal life" (Jn 3:16).

If you are to accept by faith in the revealed word of God the reality that upon your earthly death there will be a new type of existence awaiting you, then you must reflect upon that revelation. But God's revelation, both about the fact of immortal life after death for all human persons and about the nature of that life, was a gradual revelation among his chosen people of Israel, as recorded in the Old Testament, and then among his people of the new covenant as recorded in the New Testament. Let us examine this gradual revelation that comes to us through a prayerful consideration of the pages of the Old and New Testaments.

Sheol

The Hebrew word *Sheol* means "abyss." Up to a century and a half before Christ's coming the Jews held a view of Sheol that was similarly found among the Persians, Egyptians, Greeks and Latins. Below the earth existed a dark, gloomy cavern. All souls went there, both the good and the bad. The primitive thought among the Jews did not distinguish degrees of retribution meted out for deeds performed while living. The good went there in peace and tranquillity after a long, prosperous, earthly life while evil persons were snatched from earthly existence by an untimely fate. Existence there was described as dreamy, dark and silent. But the central point is that there was belief in some sort of life after death.

Job describes the land of Sheol:

. . .leave me a little joy,
before I go to the place of no return,
the land of murk and deep shadow,
where dimness and disorder hold sway,
and the light itself is like the dead of night
     (Jb 10:20-22).

In Sheol there is no remembrance of Yahweh. "Who can sing your praises in Sheol?" (Ps 6:5).

Hades

During the second and first centuries B.C. the Septuagint translated *Sheol* into the Greek word *Hades.* Under the influence of apocalyptic literature, especially coming from Zoroaster's *Zend-Avesta,* and the apocalyptic books of Enoch (written about 200 B.C.) and Ezra, Jewish teachers began to distinguish between the good and the evil ones who entered Hades. The good were rewarded by going to a blissful, joyful part of Hades called *Paradise.* Evil persons immediately upon death began their suffering punishment in the part of Hades that eventually in the intertestamentary period was called *Gehenna.*[1]

Resurrection

The good persons in the upper part of Hades awaited the day of resurrection in peace and joy. The doctrine of the resurrection of the just, at this time of Jewish religious development, came into popular thinking as we see beautifully and dramatically expressed in chapter seven of 2 Maccabees. The seven brothers who are to be martyred are exhorted by their mother to remain loyal to Yahweh in the hope of a future resurrection. The fourth son expresses this belief: ". . .yet relying on God's promise that we shall be raised up by him; whereas for you there can be no resurrection, no new life" (2 Mc 7:14).

The division of Hades into two sections is used by Luke in the parable of Lazarus and Dives. The apocalyptic book of Enoch describes the two parts of Hades:

> Such a division has been made for the spirits of the righteous, in which there is the bright spring of water. And such has been made for sinners when they die and are buried in the earth and judgment has not been executed on them in their lifetime. Here their spirits shall be set apart in the great pain till the great day of judgment and punishment and torment of those who curse for ever, and retribution for their spirits. There he shall bind them for ever.[2]

No doubt Luke refers to this popular belief as Dives asks Lazarus to dip his finger into the water to cool his burning tongue.

Gehenna

Gehenna, known to all Jews who visited Jerusalem, including Jesus, as the valley of Hinnom, was the city garbage heap that burned day and night. In the time of

King Ahaz and Manasseh, children were sacrificed to the pagan god, Baal. Isaiah describes it as a place of punishment for the wicked dead (Is 66:24). For some time Hades was the intermediate state of punishment for the wicked who would then be eternally condemned to unquenchable fire in Gehenna.

This is undoubtedly the understanding of Hades as hell, an intermediate state of two divisions that allowed the early Christians to assert in their creeds as we still do in the Apostles' Creed: ". . . and he (Jesus) suffered, died and descended into hell. . . ." Have you ever asked yourself what does Christ's descent into hell mean? The author of St. Peter's first epistle has this Jewish understanding of Hades in mind when he writes: "In the body he was put to death, in the spirit he was raised to life, and in the spirit he went to preach to the spirits in prison" (1 Pt 3:18-19).

The early Fathers are unanimous in believing that Jesus, upon his death on the cross, descended into the subterranean place of Hades or hell and there preached to the dead. "The dead had to be told the Good News as well, so that though, in their life on earth, they had been through the judgment that comes to all humanity, they might come to God's life in the spirit" (1 Pt 4:6).

These texts show us a common belief in the first century of Christianity that was so highly influenced in its language and imagery by Jewish apocalyptic literature. This was known to Jesus himself who used it, however, in a more spiritual meaning than in the manner in which even his disciples most likely understood it. Hades or hell is an intermediate state for the just and the unjust who both wait for a final judgment. Gradually, the intermediate and final state for the evil ones are both called Gehenna and this is hell as Jesus refers to it several times (Mt 5:22; 8:12; 10:28; 25:46; Mk 9:43,48; Lk 12:5).[3]

Gehenna now becomes the metaphorical name for hell, an underground region of fire where the damned are punished after death. Paradise is the immediate state of blissful happiness where the just enter to receive eternal life before the final resurrection when they shall enter into the fullness of eternal life called heaven. St. Luke presents Christ as accepting the teachings of the Pharisees of his time on Gehenna and paradise as two distinct regions of punishment and reward for the unjust and the just after death, with a final resurrection given only to the just at the end of time which would allow the just to enter into eternal heaven.

This can be seen in St. Luke in the parable of Lazarus and Dives (Lk 16:19), the promise of Jesus to the good thief that he would enter immediately upon death into paradise (Lk 23:43) and in the description of St. Stephen enjoying life with Christ immediately after death (Acts 7:59). In these three cases the New Testament writer teaches us the distinction between Gehenna as a fiery place of punishment for the unjust and paradise as a happy abode for the just who immediately upon death live in Christ.

Judgment

Thus we see in Scripture the belief that there is life after death and there are divisions of human beings into the just and the unjust. For the just who love and obey God there is an immediate entrance into bliss and joy called paradise. For the unjust there is immediate retribution and punishment in Gehenna or hell. From such distinctions of persons and places of reward or punishment we can deduce that implicitly, at least, some judgment is given to each person at the moment of death, depending on how that person has lived his or her life on earth.

The early writers of the Old Testament pictured God

as passing judgment on human lives before death oc-
curred. God judged a person by his or her desires and actions to be pleasing to him and hence he rewarded man
and woman with the signs of approbation: a long and
prosperous life with a great posterity. Evil persons were
judged by God for their wickedness according to the signs
of sudden death, an impoverished life and no descen-
dants (cf. Jb 15:20-21; Ps 140: 12; Wis 3-5).

The New Testament writers indicate more definitely
but still implicitly that a separation between the good and
evil persons occurs at the time of death when they are
assigned to hell or paradise. This we have seen in the
parable of Lazarus and Dives (Lk 16:19-31). St. John the
Baptist continually exhorts his listeners to repentance
since there will be a "winnowing" that will separate the
wheat from the chaff (Mt 3:12); the ax will be put to the
tree and the fruitless tree will be cut down and cast into
the fire (Lk 3:9).

Jesus preaches a state of constant vigilance since the
Master will return and have a reckoning (Lk 12:35ff.).
People must enter by the narrow door (Lk 13:24) and
that door will soon be closed. The wicked ones who did
not enter will be cast out, where "there will be weeping
and grinding of teeth" (Lk 13:28).

Still we see in the New Testament a clear teaching of
a final judgment that goes beyond the individual judgment. Yet the individual judgment is at the matrix of the
general judgment at the end of the world. There will be a
final sifting of the wheat from the thistles, the sheep will
be separated from the goats, the unfruitful fig tree will be
cut down and burnt.

Matthew's Gospel brings to a dramatic climax the
New Testament teaching on the last judgment (Mt
25:31-46). We see a definitive judgment passed on each
person, depending on how he or she loved and served
Christ in his members. Such a final judgment puts the ac-

cent more on the glorification of the Body of Christ. Yet such a relation of any individual person to the whole Christ in glory is dependent on that person's individual judgment that he passes on himself at the end of his earthly life. More will be developed on this theme in a later chapter. Our concentration now concerns the intermediate state between death and the final resurrection.

Possible Growth

Before we can work out a more viable view of the intermediate state of persons between death and the end of the world, we need to ask whether scripture gives us any teaching or even hint concerning a possible growth in such an interim period. If you are judged and directed toward hell or paradise in accordance with how you have lived your life on earth, can there be any change in that judgment? If there is no room for growth in the intermediate state, then what does the final judgment add? Even for those who are justified and die in Christ, is there not a need for the healing of past habits, relationships, ways of looking at God, themselves, others and the whole world? Even though the good thief entered into paradise, was he not in need of a bit of therapy to prepare himself for the full enjoyment of heaven? Can the prayers of the faithful living in the Church Militant not aid such persons?

Purgatory

There is no explicit teaching in scripture about purgatory or the state where we human beings can be cleansed from the traces of sin in our members (Rom 7:23). Some biblical scholars in times past have used St. Paul's teaching found in 1 Corinthians 3:11-15 to establish such a doctrine. St. Paul declares that our work in this life "is going to be clearly revealed when the day comes. That day will begin with fire, and the fire will test the quality of each man's work." But this does not seem to support the doctrine of purgatory.

Such a doctrine can be seen only as an evolution of the church's sense, (1) that the prayers of the faithful on earth can help those who have died and entered into a new spiritual existence and (2) that our call by God to be perfect and fulfilled according to his own image and likeness is a process that in the majority of cases is not finished in this life. The second point is quite evident. Few human beings reach perfect fulfillment in this earthly existence. The first point, based on Christ's charge given his apostles to teach and hence to open up the revelation he gave to his church, needs a fuller development that will be found in Chapters 3 and 4.

In regard to the constant practice in both the Eastern and Western Churches of offering prayers, sacrifices and, above all, the Divine Liturgy to help the deceased, there can be no doubt that the church believed liturgically in the communion of saints and the intercommunion between members of the Body of Christ still living on earth who can come to the aid of the injured members of the Church Suffering.

Some of the early Fathers appeal to the action of Judas in 2 Maccabees 12:38-45 as a scriptural affirmation that the living may help the deceased. He had his people refrain from sin on behalf of his fallen soldiers and he sent 2,000 drachmae to Jerusalem. "This was why he had this atonement sacrifice offered for the dead, so that they might be released from their sin" (2 Mc 12:45).

Such a widespread practice of the living offering prayers and sacrifices on behalf of the deceased is clearly attested to in the writings of Tertullian, Origen, Cyprian, Ephraem, Ambrose, Augustine, Chrysostom, Basil, Gregory of Nazianzus, Gregory of Nyssa and Gregory the Great. It is found in the liturgical services in the East and

West from the earliest texts as well as carved on the tomb-stones to remind the living on earth to pray for the deceased.

Such common, universal practice can be implicitly and cogently supported by studying both how God works in the order of salvation according to laws of progressive growth and how we human beings are formed for good or evil by a society in which there is mutual communication. That there should be an interim period of "cleansing" and therapy in which God can continue his merciful work of healing us harmonizes with God's manner throughout all of the history of salvation as seen in Sacred Scripture.

Laws of Growth

God works in the material creation of this universe according to a law of growth and development. How much more he works in our spiritual development, slowly and progressively, ever revealing himself where two or three gather in love. God gradually revealed himself to us as love over thousands of years, as he spoke his word in the hearts of peoples of all cultures. But "when the appointed time came, God sent his Son, born of a woman, born a subject of the Law, to redeem the subjects of the Law and to enable us to be adopted as sons" (Gal 4:4-6).

But evil was not cast out once God's Word became flesh. Jesus died and rose from the dead and in his resurrected life he can pour the Holy Spirit into our hearts, whereby we can know God as our Father, Abba, and believe we are truly his children and heirs of heaven (Rom 8:15, Gal 4:6). Such an awareness is a progressive development of consciousness to be developed in daily events. When have you in your lifetime on earth considered yourself completely "dead to sin but alive for God in Christ Jesus" (Rom 6:11)?

God has made you according to his own image and

likeness (Gn 1:26), that is, Jesus Christ. This growth "in Christ," which St. Paul writes of 164 times, is a long, slow process. Why should God's "justifying" or divinizing process be limited only to this earthly existence? St. Paul speaks of becoming true images of God's Son:

> They are the ones he chose specially long ago and intended to become true *images* of his Son, so that his Son might be the eldest of many brothers. He called those he intended for this; those he called he justified, and with those he justified he shared his glory (Rom 8:29-30).

Can you assert that even a full lifetime as a Christian is sufficient to accomplish this? You are to strive to be perfect as your heavenly Father is perfect. For this end God is always working, always loving you. He does not cease to love you and work to bring you into greater oneness with his Son, Jesus, in order to share more of his trinitarian life. His love and mercy endure forever and that means they are operative always even in the life after death. For God's love and mercy are always active and they transcend the limitations of space and time.

A Just God

From scripture we know that God has created *all* of us to share his life and happiness: not only Christians, not only adults, but children who have died prematurely, the retarded, and people in certain societies that do not permit a full free life to evolve. Of the 40 million people who die annually, the majority do not know Jesus Christ, the fullness of God's expressed love for mankind. Can God's salvific will be tied to the conditions of this earthly existence?

God's goodness and holiness must continue to manifest themselves in the life to come. So many of our relationships have never developed to a point where we found God's presence shining diaphanously through them. Why would God cease to shine through such relationships in the life to come when we and others still retain the same personhood as in this earthly existence with a built-in avidity to continue to grow in even more unifying love relationships?

If God has wished to reveal his presence as love in those few persons whom you, in God's providence, have been privileged to love in this life, can you not believe that it is most basic to scripture that God wants in the life to come to reveal his beauty and love through every human person and angel ever created and evolved into true uniqueness by God's special, loving activity in that life?

I would like to develop more at length this intermediate state of continued growth in the next chapter. Let me now bring together in summary form what I believe God has revealed to us about the intermediate stage between death and the final judgment.

My first conclusion must be that scripture, including the specific teaching of Jesus, is much more concerned with accentuating the present life with the necessity of living well *now* than in stressing details about what happens immediately after death. Jesus, above all, was a masterful teacher and knew the human heart. He knew all too well how easily we tend to postpone what is now possible in the light of theorizing about a nebulous future. But his great message centers upon the reality that our future life grows out of the person we become through this life's choices.

We are the bundle of relationships developed in this life. We carry such relationships into the life to come. Hence this present life is really the only important "place" where we freely determine what type of life we would enjoy in the next life.

Jesus, as a teacher, in speaking of future states after death, accentuates more the ultimate states of heaven and hell and the final consummation because, being ultimate and definitive, these should have greater impact pedagogically on his listeners than descriptions of intermediate states.

Unbroken Continuity

From God's revelation in Holy Scripture and the church's teaching we see that immediately after death we continue to exist as conscious beings with the same personhood, with all the moral and spiritual attainments or lack of the same that we acquired or failed to acquire while on earth. Scripture shows Moses and Elias speaking to Jesus in the Transfiguration scene and each retaining his unique personality (1 Pt 3:18-20). In Jesus' parable of Lazarus and Dives (Lk 16:19-31) the two retain consciousness in the life after death with their past attitudes. These come forth and exert a rewarding or punishing effect on each person.

We will live and think and speak according to the values that we have appreciated and lived by during this life. Jesus insisted: "For where your treasure is, there will your heart be also" (Mt 6:21; Lk 12:34). As one sows, thus one reaps.

Following this thought of an unbroken continuity in the same consciousness, we can thus better interpret whatever Scripture or the church has taught about reward and punishment immediately given for our good or bad deeds. St. Paul writes: "For all the truth about us will be brought out in the law court of Christ, and each of us will get what he deserves for the things he did in the body, good or bad" (2 Cor 5:10).

It is not that our deeds are extrinsic to us, things we have done as symbols of our love or indifference toward

God, and for them we are rewarded or punished. It is more that within our own daily experiences we become our choices. It is true that we inherit many characteristics from our parents. Society can precondition us toward certain values and ways of conduct. But all of these influences are precisely a part of our daily experiences, our *actuality* or being-in-the-world. It is, therefore, in the human, existential context that we acquire our set of personal characteristics that make ourselves who or what we are by our daily decisions of lack of decision (which in itself is a decision) to act out of self-forgetting love or self-centered narcissism.

To present life after death as a reward for good works done on earth can be a subtle temptation toward self-centeredness. We do good deeds for others, not because we truly love them, but because such persons are used by us as an occasion for avoiding hell (punishment) and enjoying heaven (all the nice things we ever had on earth but infinitely more glorious and never-ending!). We *do* in order to *receive* something. But in reality our choices make us *to be* what we are. This changes our view of a judgment after death.

Judgment

We can never really perform an action that ultimately remains "neutral." We can only choose what will eventually lead toward selfishness (Mammon) or toward self-transcendence (God). Our daily choices move us to a final yes or no, to a loving obedience to God or a turning away from him in our bias toward self. We truly make a final option on our deathbed, but it has been preconditioned by all our preceding choices.

Thus in a way we,not God, judge ourselves in the life to come. We "send" ourselves to such a state of hellish self-absorption, isolation from others, lack of any true identity received in loving relationships toward others. We also prepare ourselves for the kingdom of heaven by allowing God to be central in our choices. When God sits in judgment what he really is doing is reading the verdict that we have passed on the gift of life he gave us. God allows us to see what we have chosen. We see God through Jesus Christ in his Spirit of love and we see the person that our choices have made us to be.

C.S. Lewis in *The Last Battle* has all the creatures of Narnia pass through the door of the stable which is death. All of them must face Aslan, the Lion. As they do, some of them look at him in fear and hatred and they depart to the left into the black shadow of Aslan and are not seen or heard of again. Others, however, "looked in the face of Aslan and loved him, though some of them were very frightened at the same time."[4]

In this life we can fail to make decisions according to the standard of Jesus Christ. We can avoid looking into his face and making our decisions out of love for him. But after death we will see his face and know that our choices have made us "true images" of him (Rom 8:29) or not.

Christ's Meaning

We have seen how much of New Testament eschatology (concerning life after death) is tied to imagery and doctrine derived from Jewish and Persian apocalyptic literature. Zoroaster, centuries before Christ, taught concerning a Messiah who would come at the end of time to inaugurate the messianic age. Both the Jews and Persians taught a Sheol that was literally believed to be under the world. St. Paul preached that Jesus Christ had conquered sin and death. This is not the physical death, for both he and all succeeding human beings would die, but it is the death of the deceased having to go into Hades, the world of gloom and darkness.

Jesus risen makes it possible by "descending" to "ascend" by leading us out of the death of Hades to the true life in him. "When he ascended to the height, he captured prisoners, he gave gifts to men" (Eph 4:8). St. Paul and many of his contemporaries believed that Jesus would actually return in glory to their earth within their own lifetime. Thus the writers of the New Testament as well as the early Fathers who commented on it all too often believed in the literalness of the images used.

But Jesus, who borrowed such images familiar to all his listeners, used them as metaphors to relay his real teaching. Jesus was not interested in telling the future. He preached in order to convert persons to the love of his Father. If he described hell in apocalyptic imagery of inextinguishable fire and darkness and suffocating brimstone, it was not to give facts of a concrete, existing place of fiery punishment. He sought by such details to speak to human wills and move them away from the burning, gnawing darkness of selfishness to the light of his transcendent risen presence in their lives.

The details of the afterlife for Jesus are not of primary importance. What alone matters is that God has to be supreme. Only then can there be true life. Life alone is important, not death. "I have come so that they may have life and have it to the full" (Jn 10:10).

The following chapters that deal with purgatory, hell and heaven are meant to call the reader to serious reflection on the essential aspects of these teachings from Scripture and the church's teaching. By moving away from a literal understanding of the imagery so widely used in revelation, the reader can come to a more real understanding of life after death. Above all, you can thus be challenged to see your present life as the important, determining factor for your life after death.

Our modern age, from Scholasticism of the 12th century to the present, is obsessed with the desire to prove the immortality of the soul and the existence of life after death. Jesus would have us not worry about such things, but to believe that his risen life is now available to all who accept it. For such, Hades does not exist, only heaven which is already a reality for those who live even now in Christ Jesus. By obedience and faith, purity of heart and holiness, we now accept a share in Jesus who truly nullifies the hold of the underworld over us.

This important truth is highlighted in the theological message seen in the icon of Christ's resurrection according to Byzantine iconography. Jesus risen is seen pulling an old man out of the bowels of the earth. Around such an icon Byzantine Christians sing triumphantly this hymn for 50 days after Easter:

> Christ is risen from the dead,
> trampling down death by death
> and granting life to those in
> the tomb.

He is *now* fulfilling the visions of The Book of Revelation:

> Do not be afraid, it is I, the *First*
> and the *Last,* I am the Living One, I
> was dead and now I am to live for ever
> and ever, and I hold the keys of death
> and of the underworld (Rv 1:17-18).

Eternal Life

Jesus, therefore, used the images and prevalent teachings of his time, not to give us facts that our intellectual curiosity could feed on, but in order to convey his deeper, more spiritual truths. It is we who have objectified his poetic, metaphorical language to develop a world of future life after death, of hell and heaven as places to receive things as punishments and rewards for good deeds done on earth. It is we who have disembodied the soul and placed it after death in a time and space perspective with the hope that our souls will one day be literally rejoined with the bodies that now "rest" in some grave.

His teaching insists strongly on the importance of your living this temporal life on a spiritual plane. After death, you, a whole person, enter into a spiritual world. You retain your personhood developed by your choices in this life. But heaven can already be a life in that spiritual world lived on this earth as you surrender to the divine indwelling presence of the risen Lord. Dying, as Jesus saw it in his own life, is a going home to the Father. It is an ongoing process of letting that life within you grow through loving relationships lived now and continued in the life to come.

The keys over death and the underworld that he holds out to you are a daily invitation to share in his eternal life by denying yourself in this life, taking up your cross and following him to greater life by the love you have for the Father and by the humble service you show in extending that love to all your brothers and sisters.

Chapter Five
Purgatory: Healing Therapy

In the Charles Williams novel, *All Hallows Eve,* we are treated to a view of the afterlife. Enforced by his deep Christian faith, Williams offers a profound grasp of the theological tradition of a life of growth after death, and a penetrating understanding of human psychology.

In the novel, two women friends named Lester and Evelyn die in an auto crash. The main plot centers on the relationships of these two women with a mutual friend from their school days, named Betty. Betty is caught between the effects of a loving goodness shown to her by Lester and the evil shown to her by Evelyn. With keen theological insight, the author shows how the deceased Lester comes to the living Betty, seeking forgiveness so that she may receive peace and joy in her eternal life. Betty gives the forgiveness for the small slights Lester had shown her in their school days.

> The tears came into Lester's eyes, but this time they did not fall. Betty's figure swam indistinctly before her and then she blinked the tears away. They looked at each other and Betty laughed and Lester found herself beginning to laugh, but as she did so she exclaimed, "All the same—!" Betty put out her

> hand toward the other's lips, as if to hush her,
> but it did not reach them. Clear though they
> had become, and freely though they shared
> in that opening City a common good, still its
> proper definitions lay between them. The
> one was dead, the other not. The *Noli me
> tangere* of the City's own Lord Mayor was, in
> their small degree, imposed on them. Betty's
> hand dropped gently to her side. They half
> recognized the law and courteously yielded
> to it. [1]

This story stirs within us many interesting questions.
After death are we able to be in touch with those still living, especially our friends? Can we grow in any way in
the life to come? Can others on earth or those already in
the afterlife come to our help? Are we able to be in contact with other deceased persons? What sort of punishment awaits us if there is a state of purification? How long
does it last?

I have already raised and partially answered some of
these questions. We must now look more in depth at the
intermediate state of those who die and do not immediately reach a state of heaven or hell. This is what
Catholics call *purgatory*. The Orthodox accept such a
state but in general do not use the same term. Let us,
then, first review the church's teaching on purgatory as it
evolved through history so that we can reflect on a less
legalistic, more interpersonal view of purgatory, a view
seen as healing therapy.

Catholic Teaching

Scripture scholars do not agree that the doctrine of
purgatory is explicitly found in Holy Scripture.
Nonetheless, certain scriptural passages have provided
some Fathers and theologians with the occasion for
discoursing on this third condition. Chief among these

texts are 2 Maccabees 12:45-46: "But if he did this with a view to the splendid reward that awaits those who had gone to rest in godliness, it was a holy and pious thought. Thus he made atonement for the dead that they might be freed from this sin";[2] and 1 Cor 3:13-15: ". . .the work of each will be made clear. . . fire will test the quality of each man's work. . . if a man's building burns, he will suffer loss. He himself will be saved, but only as one fleeing through fire."[3]

However, we can say that there is no explicit doctrine of purgatory in the Old or New Testament. Yet these texts would be used to support the doctrine that gradually developed from the early church's universal practice of offering prayers, alms and the Divine Liturgy (a term used for Mass in the Eastern Church) on behalf of the departed. Such a practice is found in all the liturgies and funeral services in ancient times. Typical of such liturgical prayers is the litany for the dead as found in the liturgy of St. John Chrysostom.

> Let us pray also for the repose of the souls of the departed servants of God and for the forgiveness of their every transgression, deliberate and indeliberate. . . . The mercies of God, the kingdom of Heaven and the remission of their sins let us ask of Christ, our immortal King and our God. . . . God of spirits and of all flesh, who has trampled on death and vanquished the devil and given life to Your world, give rest, O Lord, to the souls of Your departed servants in a place of light, a place of refreshment, a place of repose, from which pain, sorrow and sighing have fled. Because You are so good and love mankind, forgive their every offense, whether in word or deed or thought; for there is no man living and never will be who does not sin: but You alone are without sin. . . .

We find this universal practice of praying for the departed in the writings of the early Fathers, both of the East and the West, such as Tertullian, Origen, Ephraem, Cyprian, Ambrose, Augustine, Basil, Gregory of Nazianzus, Gregory of Nyssa, John Chrysostom and Pope Gregory the Great.

This belief in the power of prayer to help the departed is attested to by the inscriptions found on tombstones. The departed beg for a remembrance and for prayers of their loved ones still living so that God might grant them a place of peace and rest.

The early Fathers seemed to have developed a teaching that only the very holy, such as apostles, martyrs and prophets, entered immediately into a heavenly reward, while the ordinary Christians were in need of some sort of cleansing and healing from the legacy of sin. St. Gregory of Nyssa writes that: ". . .after the departure from the body (a soul that is not purified) . . .will not be able to participate in divinity, unless the cleansing fire will have purged away all stains on the soul."[4]

In the West St. Augustine developed a very concrete doctrine of purgatory, based on his interpretation of 1 Cor 3:11-15. From him we receive the notion of a place to which those not yet purified must go to be purified by a cleansing fire in order to expiate for the temporal punishment due to forgiven mortal sins and for venial sins not explicitly forgiven.[5]

Those in the West who developed further the doctrine of purgatory accentuated St. Augustine's legalistic approach. In the East, however, the existence of purgatory and the accent on making "satisfaction" through temporal punishments by fire were never well-defined or separated from the teaching of hell. Drawing from Holy Scripture, patristic homilies, liturgical services, the lives of the Saints and certain revelations and visions of life after death, the Eastern writers describe a state of healing therapy, brought about by the prayers of the church and individuals, especially as presented in the Divine Liturgy.

Thus we can say that the early Fathers in the East and West do not strive to prove the existence of an intermediate state of purification but they take it for granted because of the widespread practice of prayers and the liturgy offered in order to help the departed.[6] The Councils of the church, especially the reunion Councils of Lyons II (1274) and of Florence (1439), that unsuccessfully aimed at uniting the Western Catholic and the Eastern Orthodox Churches, unanimously agreed that there is a state of purgatory and that the prayers of the faithful on earth can help those departed who are in need of cleansing and healing.[7]

New Views

Theologians today are taking a fresh look at traditional teaching about purgatory. They question the accent placed on the soul separated from the body, then imprisoned and subjugated to a punishment of fire that is not only the pain of sense, but the pain of the damned—the temporary privation of the vision of God. Legalism, inherited from St. Augustine, distinguishes between *reatus poenae* (burden of punishment due to sin that needs "satisfaction," Augustine's main reason for the existence of purgatory) and *reatus culpae* (the guilt incurred).

More aware today of the human person as a whole being, both in this earthly existence and in the life to come, such modern thinkers reject the separation of body and soul after death. The whole person continues to exist with the same consciousness of personhood as he or she acquired in his or her earthly life. We have already pointed out Karl Rahner's teaching of the whole person in death attaining a holistic (body-soul-spirit relationship), all-cosmic relationship to the world.

When Rahner speaks of the punishment in purgatory, he sees it as part of a further maturing of the individual after death. We should no longer imagine God vindictively heaping punishment upon us. Rather we become the source of punishment because of our free choices made on earth that have caused disharmony in God's right order.

Rahner writes:

> . . .purgatory comes to mean, plausibly, that the soul, after surrendering her concrete bodily structure and, indeed, through that act of surrender, comes in her free, active and morally self-determining state, to experience acutely her own harmony or disharmony with the objectively right order of the world and even, by this fresh appreciation, to contribute positively to the establishment of that right order. . . .[8]

A Maturing Process

Surely we can all understand that few human beings in their lifetimes will have succeeded in their relationships to God, fellow human beings and the world around them, and reached their full potential as human persons.

So often such inadequacies come from other outside forces influencing us. We may die opting for God, yet such a choice has not filtered into the unconscious where strata upon strata of human experience have been stored up from our earthly life. They have not been fully penetrated by divine life and have not been brought consciously into the life of the Risen Christ.

Rahner again describes purgatory well, as a "full ripening" of the whole person after death:

> The many dimensions of man do not all attain their perfection simultaneously and

hence there is a full ripening of the whole
man "after death," as his basic decision
penetrates the whole extent of this reality. In
this concept. . . the remission of punishment
(is not) a mere abstention from punishing but
rather. . . the process of painful integration of
the whole of man's stratified being into the
definitive decision about his life, taken under
the grace of God. . . We cannot indeed picture to ourselves how in particular such a process of maturing can develop in different
ways in the life after death; but *that* such a
thing is conceivable will be very difficult to
dispute a priori.[9]

A Letting Go

In this life you know how difficult it is to let go and let
God have complete control over your life. Yet your
perception of the *all-ness* of God and his immense love
for you individually can be dimmed by your readiness to
be distracted through the cares and anxieties, the tinsel
and baubles of this world. Death brings you into a new
awareness of the beauty of God and his immense love for
you. In the light of his penetrating love, you more in-
tensely realize the darkness within yourself. You become
your own punishment as you now see your arrogant ingratitude, spirit of independence, gross pride and self-
centeredness before the humble, self-sacrificing love of
the Trinity.[10]

The emptying love of God for you, especially in
Christ Jesus and his Spirit, that has been operating at
every moment of your life, now pours over you. In consciously experiencing such divine goodness, shame, sorrow and compunction fill your heart. Thus great joy and
pain coexist. The burning sensation of fire searing
through your whole being and in detail over every selfish

experience combines in a confused way with a cooling, joyful presence of God's all-pervading love.

The keen realization of what your personal sins have done to the crucified Christ must be especially painful. You come to understand in an agonizing sorrow that your selfishness, hatred and indifference toward others have truly contributed to the suffering of the total Christ, His Body. Then Christ's words in Mt 25:31-46 will sear through you and sorrow for indifference to those in need will be both a pain and a healing.

No doubt the indifference of others toward you, especially those whom you considered to be your loved ones, must also be a source of pain. You will understand more clearly your great need for your loved ones to aid you in healing your relationships with them, and yet you often see their lack of concern.

God's Love

In this life the Holy Spirit is poured over you, stirring you to great compunction and even fear for your own sinfulness and yet filling you with intense love for God because of his infinite love for you. How much more is that Spirit of love operating in the purgatorial healing? The Holy Spirit reveals to you through the Good News that "For our sakes God made him who did not know sin, to be sin, so that in him we might become the very holiness of God" (2 Cor 5:21). You begin to understand the *kenosis* of God the Father who pours his whole being into his Son. That Son, at every moment of your life on earth, has been loving you unto death in order to image the eternal Father's love for you. Such love, more than any other factor, will be the healing therapy needed to uproot your selfishness. A Belgian theologian, Piet Fransen, describes this purifying love of God:

It is his love that causes our greatest pain,

pain far greater than any we can bear on
earth. It scorches up in us all the remnants of
our self-love, ingratitude and refusal. But at
the same time it penetrates us totally which is
why purgatory is also a joy more intense than
anything we can experience on earth.[11]

Human Love

One of the purifying effects of purgatory will be to
enlighten you as to the unity of God's love for you and
other human beings (and also of angels). You will
understand God's unique and independent love for you.
But you will also experience how God has incarnated his
loving gift of self to you through the love of Jesus Christ,
then his mother Mary, the great saints and angels, and
then in the particular, loving friends that he has given
you.

Your heart will yearn to stretch out toward your
loved ones and to complete those loving friendships. And
yet any self-centeredness will flame out in your painful
recognition of the lack of love you showed them in the
past as well as your agonizing inability to love them as
you ought.

You will understand also how indifferent you were,
through prejudices, fears, ignorance and simple sinful
selfishness, toward so many persons sent into your life to
love, or at least to help in kindnesses, and whom you
turned away. You will realize that your so-called enemies
were really a part of Christ's Body and also a vital part of
you. Such lack of unity will be painful and healing as you
seek eagerly to make amends for any dissension you may
have responsibly brought into the Body of Christ.

Helped by Prayers

Now, you can see why the church's strong belief and
practice that the prayers of those on earth can benefit the

departed in purgatory. Prayers become an expressed communication of love toward another, expressed to God on behalf of the one praying. In no mechanistic, magical way are those in purgatory aided by the prayers of their loved ones on earth.

You stretch out in your loneliness and self-centeredness, like a person in prison stretches through the barred windows to contact help outside, to be called into "being" by a loved one recognizing and loving you by prayerfully recalling you. Love alone heals. For this healing of your life's hurts you need to experience God's love localized in the gifts of your loved ones. When they, who still walk this earth, lovingly remember you, you are called out of the tomb of isolation and loneliness into a new-founded state of self-identity. The healing power of love consists in the therapy of destroying isolation and building a community (a oneness, a togetherness in loving union).

When others love you and want to be present to you, even though death separates you, you experience a true finding of yourself, an expansion of your self-identity and a growth in complexity-consciousness. This is surely true in this life. Not only do you feel your inward being has expanded, but you experience an openness to the outside world, a sense of greater solidarity that allows you to be of fulfilling service to others. In true, unselfish human love, you approach closest to timelessness, to the eternal now of God's unselfish divine love. You become aware of a new level of existence, still rooted in a material existence, that transcends the temporal. You move into a consciousness that you feel could know no fatigue and no end of growth. True love, by its nature, is always creating within us a new capacity for greater love. At the same time it means a new capacity of *being* to give ourselves to another, and a new capacity to receive *being* from the one loved.

Offering the Divine Liturgy

From ancient times the Eastern and Western churches have taught that the best way to help persons in purgatory is the offering of the Divine Liturgy. Tertullian writes of anniversary Masses offered on behalf of the deceased.[12] He exhorts a widow to pray for her deceased husband, begging repose for him and "to have the Holy Sacrifice offered up for him every year on the day of his death."[13]

The Council of Trent summarizes this ancient tradition: ". . .the souls detained there (in purgatory) are helped by the suffrages of the faithful and principally by the acceptable Sacrifice of the Altar."[14]

The Divine Liturgy is the enactment in human time of the eternal *now* sacrifice of Jesus Christ offered to the Heavenly Father on behalf of the living and the dead.

Jesus Christ is always dying on behalf of each person. His intercessory power is illimitable for he is the Son of God interceding for his human brothers and sisters whether they be in the Church Militant (those still on this earth), the Church Suffering (those in purgatory) or the Church Triumphant (those in heaven). The church through the liturgy extends the sacrifice of Christ that takes away sins, and prays that God may pardon and purify the deceased persons of all their sins. To understand the value of offering liturgies for the deceased and of assisting fervently at the celebration, we must understand that the church is in the most intimate union with Christ. He is the head; we are his members.

We enter by faith into the eternal life of the triune God, but specifically, through the Incarnation, death and resurrection of Christ, we are one with him who is the resurrection and the life. We are privileged in the celebration of the Divine Liturgy to offer our particular prayers for the departed with those of the universal church. In this way we apply the fruits of redemption to those drying out in purgatory for the healing love of Christ and their loved ones.

The love that releases the infinite love of Christ for the beloved deceased depends upon our "consociating" with Christ by putting on his mind. The more you offer liturgies and prayers for the deceased and surrender yourself to Christ by expressing love for your beloved departed, the greater will be the "application" of Christ's merits for them.

The liturgy and the prayers that you offer for a beloved deceased are never static, magical moments, but are beginning points of a love process whereby you with Christ live the sacrifice of the cross in your daily life. To live the liturgy is the best way of helping your beloved departed. It directs the love of Christ unto death, along with our similar, conjoined love unto death, toward the suffering ones in purgatory.

Thus almsgiving or any other sacrifices offered up on behalf of your loved ones in purgatory are as meaningful as a part of living the Eucharistic sacrifice of unselfish love. It is this that heals the broken ones in purgatory.

Is Purgatory a Place?

If purgatory is not a vindictive punishment meted out by God to extract satisfaction for the human violations of his laws, then you can see it cannot be a place in space. It becomes a condition or state of being fashioned by the individual during his or her lifetime on earth.

Martin Jugie writes:

> It can be said that Purgatory is where the soul in Purgatory is. The suffering soul brings with it its Purgatory, just as the blessed soul takes with it the Heaven from which it can never be separated.[15]

Such a description, however, leaves out the existential reality that in the life after death you cannot exist as a static entity. Rather, you exist in the context of harmonious or disharmonious relations to those persons and created things that have shaped you. In the conscious awareness of such relationships are found the "localization" or the "place" where punishment and purifying healing take place.[16]

Is There Fire?

The punishment can, therefore, be seen as caused, in the words of Karl Rahner, "by the collision of the guilty act with the given structures of the 'exterior' established by God into which the guilt engraves itself. . . ."[17] In this sense the traditional church teaching on expiation for sins and God's justice being accomplished has a value, not in a legalistic way, but as a description of an existential process of further maturing. Such maturing, by overcoming past bad habits, correcting ignorance, letting go of resentments, confronting unforgiveness deeply rooted in the unconscious, can be seen both as a self-inflicted punishment and as a healing therapy.

From the negative side you fear to let go and surrender to the loving harmony of God. From the positive side you feel joy at experiencing God's great beauty and love in the persons of the Trinity as well as in the saints and loved ones. Both can be considered a purifying effect similar, metaphorically, to fire.

Martin Jugie, one of the first Western theologians to probe the teachings of the Eastern Fathers, describes what the purgatorial fire might be:

> Is it not the very fire of love, burning in the depths of the soul, while the soul, drawn irresistibly towards its Well-Beloved, can neither reach nor see him? Stopped in its progress by an insurmountable obstacle, that

love becomes a fire, a burning sorrow, a kind
of spiritual fever, which cannot be adequately
expressed by the human word *fire*, a real
fire, a physical fire in some sense, but having
only a faint analogy with the material fire of
earth. Love can sometimes produce effects in
the human breast which recall those of
material fire. We read in the lives of certain
saints that they could not support the ardour
of the fire which the love of God kindled
within them, and to ease the burning they
would uncover their breast to the cold. Love
is strong as death; its heat as the heat of fire,
the flames of Yahweh (cf. Cant. 8:6). It is not
to be wondered at, that the soul. . . should
still feel in its inmost recesses those strange,
sorrowful longings. Such, then, is the secret
of the fire of purgatory, lighted by love, and
very different from the infernal flames, born
of despair and hate: a fire producing in some
fashion a suffering analogous to that of
earthly fire. . . .[18]

Most modern theologians would hardly agree with
Jugie's accent on a fire, "physical in some sense."
Perhaps the agonizing purifications of mystics come
closest to an idea of such a "fire."[19] St. John of the Cross
has described well the agonizing purifications undergone
by mystics, especially in the purification of the spirit as "a
living flame of love that tenderly wounds my soul in its
deepest center."[20] His is perhaps the closest description
of the sufferings of those persons in purgatory:

This dark night is an inflow of God into the
soul, which purges it of its habitual ig-
norances and imperfections, natural and
spiritual. . . . Through this contemplation,
God teaches the soul secretly and instructs it

in the perfection of love without its doing
anything, nor understanding how this happens. . . there are two reasons why this
divine wisdom is not only night and darkness
for the soul, but also affliction and torment.
First, because of the height of the divine
wisdom which exceeds the capacity of the
soul. Second, because of the soul's baseness
and impurity; and on this account it is painful, afflictive, and also dark for the soul.[21]

A Painful Joy

And yet such affliction and torment in the heart of
one in purgatory must also be accompanied by a deep joy
and peace. Such a paradox is not easily understood except in advanced cases of mystical purifications of those
who have loved others and known both the torment and
joy of sacrificing themselves for their beloved.

This joy in purgatory is described by St. Catherine of
Genoa:

I believe no happiness can be found worthy
to be compared with that of a soul in
Purgatory except that of the saints in
Paradise; and day by day this happiness
grows as God flows into these souls, more
and more as the hindrance to his entrance is
consumed. Sin's rust is the hindrance, and
the fire burns the rust away so that more and
more the soul opens itself up to the divine in-
flowing. . . . As the rust lessens and the soul
is opened up to the divine ray, happiness
grows; until the time be accomplished the
one wanes and the other waxes. . . . As for
will: never can the souls say these pains are
pains, so contented are they with God's or-
daining with which, in pure charity, their will
is united.[22]

Orthodox View

Although the Eastern churches have always insisted on an intermediate state where persons could receive help through the prayers, good works and especially the offering of the Divine Liturgy, they, nevertheless, have not been overly concerned with describing the details of such a state. One predominant insight, passed on through their long theological tradition, is the lack of distinction between hell and purgatory.

Mark of Ephesus, in his first homily delivered at the Council of Florence (1439), to refute the Latin idea of a purgatorial fire, maintains that hell and purgatory are not two separate places of differing punishments. There is only hell. He presents the common Orthodox teaching that all persons in hell can be helped by the prayers of the faithful on earth. To this end he quotes a statement that he attributes to St. Basil the Great:

> Who also, on this all-perfect and saving feast, art graciously pleased to accept propitiatory for those who are imprisoned in hell, granting us a great hope of improvement for those who are imprisoned from the defilements which have imprisoned them, and that Thou wilt send down Thy consolation (Third Kneeling Prayer at Vespers).[23]

The Orthodox cloak life after death in great mystery, but highlight the belief of the early church that prayers offered for the dead can have a salutary effect on all who die, those in heaven and those in hell (which embraces those in purgatory). In a rather long but important statement, Serge Bulgakov in 1935 summarizes the common belief of the Orthodox:

> The Church believes firmly in the real action

of these prayers. They can ameliorate the state of the souls of sinners, and liberate them from the place of distress, snatch them from hell. This action of prayer, of course, supposes not only intercession before the Creator, but a direct action on the soul, an awakening of the powers of the soul, capable of making it worthy of pardon.

The Orthodox Church does not know purgatory as a special *place* or state. There are not sufficient biblical or dogmatic foundations for asserting the existence of a third place of this nature. Nevertheless, the possibility of a *state* of purification is undeniable—an idea common to both Orthodoxy and Catholicism. From the point of view of *practical religion,* the distinction between hell and purgatory is imperceptible, for the fate of each soul beyond the tomb is completely unknown to us. What is fundamentally important is not the distinction between hell and purgatory as two different places where souls live; it is more their distinction as different *states.* This offers, consequently, the possibility of liberation from the pains of hell and of passing from an estate of reprobation to that of justification. In this sense it may be asked not if a purgatory exists, but even more if a "definitive hell" exists. In other words, is not hell a sort of purgatory? The Church at least knows no bounds to the efficacy of prayers for those who have quitted this world in union with the Church, and it believes in the effective action of these prayers.[24]

Helping Others

The persons in purgatory, as they are being purified and healed of their self-centeredness, are free to exercise the newfound love that God's Spirit has poured into their hearts. This love is shown, no doubt, toward their own loved ones, toward those who have provided them healing love and toward those who are in great spiritual need of God's love in their lives.

Although Saints and angels, filled with God's presence and purified of all selfishness, have greater power of intercession, such persons in purgatory have a God-given loyalty toward their loved ones and toward those with whom the deceased had lived and worked on earth. As such stretch out toward God in ardent intercession for their loved ones and acquaintances, new levels of heroism and love are reached.

Healing therapy is the uprooting of self-centeredness, and the very act of loving those in need, "A man can have no greater love than to lay down his life for his friends," said Jesus (Jn 15:13). As he did on the cross in imitation of the kenotic love of his heavenly Father toward each of his children, so his Holy Spirit inspires his disciples, even those in the state of purification. The only sign whereby people will recognize them as his followers is the love they have for one another, for all men. The only true sign of a newly acquired level of healing through the therapy of love received, is giving love to those who need it.

My earthly father passed away a few years ago. But God has gifted me with such a vivid realization of his living presence throughout the entire day, especially when I celebrate the Mass, that I can hardly lament the fact of his death, but praise God that he has died in the Lord and is now becoming the contemplative that God calls all of us to be. I believe I have felt his intercession on my behalf in unique ways. This, I feel, is because I allow him to exercise love toward me through his involving intercession.

Thus purgatory should no longer be a terrifying place of penal punishment. Rather, it should be seen as a place of interchange between those persons who are close to God and those in need of overcoming "neurotic" spiritual obstacles in order to be healed. In turn, those healed become loving intercessors toward the needy on earth and also toward those with them in purgatory who need their loving presence.

Purgatory is real. It is as real as all of us who, both in this life and in the life to come, have not yet surrendered every part of our being, every relationship that has made us who we are, to Jesus Christ. It is painful. It is joyful. It is learning to die. It is experiencing new levels of life in the Risen Savior. It is a vital part of heaven. It is the ante-chamber to fullness of happiness.

Chapter Six
Communion of Saints

A modern phenomenon, unparalleled in the history of mankind, is the shrinking of the world into a "global village." Satellites enable us to communicate instantly with any part of our earth. We are in physical and even psychic oneness with our brothers and sisters scattered throughout the world. We cannot shut out the cries of the poor, the destitute, the homeless alien and continue to live in selfish isolation without creating great guilt in our lives.

Technology is bringing us the preparatory means to move into a spiritual oneness. Communication precedes greater union and the end of creatures is to attain a oneness in loving union that is called communion. Love alone brings communion with another human being. It is love that brings communion with departed loved ones, along with the saints and angels in glory. But this reality is attained only through faith in the doctrine of the communion of saints as taught and practiced liturgically by the church for 2,000 years. Let us reflectively explore this ancient teaching in order to draw applications that will have important consequences in our own lives.

The Body of Christ

St. Paul was converted on the road to Damascus when Jesus spoke the words: "Saul, Saul, why are you persecuting me?" (Acts 9:4). He was told that he was persecuting Jesus when he persecuted Jesus' followers. Paul never forgot those words and his whole life as a Christian and ardent apostle could be summarized as a steady progression in understanding the meaning and implications of those words. He developed his teaching on the church from a theological study of man that he so often phrases simply as a new existence *in* or *with* Christ. It is not simply that Jesus exerts an influence upon the Christian, but that the Christian enters into an ontological oneness with Jesus, "by a change transforming him 'one man, one body' (Eph 2:15-16) into the bodily Christ."[1]

St. Paul writes:

> . . . and you are, all of you, sons of God through faith in Christ Jesus. All baptized in Christ, you have all clothed yourselves in Christ, and there are no more distinctions between Jew and Greek, slave and free, male and female, but all of you are one in Christ Jesus. Merely by belonging to Christ you are the posterity of Abraham, the heirs he was promised (Gal 3:26-29).

He could move easily, in his writings, between the levels where he found this new life in Christ in process, either in the individual or in the Christian community. He does not strictly distinguish between the building of the individual and the building of the total community, the church, since he saw them as two views of the same reality: the life of the risen Jesus Christ, living both in the individual and in the united members of his body, the church. He also was convinced that there was no true sanctity or God's life outside the organism he called the Body of Christ. As the individual Christian grew in holiness by serving his neighbor, so the Body of Christ, the church, grew in holiness.

Paul sees this gathering of human beings as a community, a *koinonia* or brotherhood, of Christian believers linked together by the bonds of faith, sacraments, especially baptism which incorporates the members into the community, and the Eucharist which symbolizes the union of the members with Christ's body, and deepens that union. There was also the bond of obedience to the appointed bishops and presbyters empowered by Christ to teach his word with his very own authority.

In this Body of Christ, just as in the human body, there are many parts; yet each has its own role in adding greater beauty and life to the whole body (1 Cor 12:12-27). Therefore, as parts of the whole, we belong to each other (Rom 12:4). ". . . so all of us, in union with Christ, form one body, and as parts of it we belong to each other" (Rom 12:5). Christ loves this body, the church, cherishing and nourishing it. ". . . it is his body—and we are its living parts" (Eph 5:30). Christ is the head of this body who nourishes and strengthens the whole body with a divine growth (Col 2:19). The whole body is dependent on Christ. Each part is knitted into the harmonious whole through the energy that comes from Jesus Christ, the source of supply. The body grows and builds itself up through love (Eph 4:16; Col 1:18; Col 1:24; Eph 1:22-23; 4:15; 5:23).

Communion of Saints

Progressively the early Christians grew in awareness of their oneness that constituted the Body of Christ. The love of the Holy Spirit that was poured out into their hearts (Rom 5:5) bound them into a loving, serving union. "There is one Body, one Spirit. . ." (Eph 4:4).

They daily experienced this loving oneness and the need to go in haste to serve the needy members of the Body of Christ.

Thus within the first five centuries of Christianity the doctrine of the communion of saints evolved. It is based on the solid belief, as we have pointed out in earlier chapters, that death does not separate the great saints, the apostles, martyrs, confessors, from those still living on earth or from those still undergoing healing therapy after death. Rather, this doctrine teaches us that all members who are in the Body of Christ, whether on earth or in the life after death, remain joined, not only to the Head, Jesus Christ, but to each member.

For our purpose it means especially that the great heroes, the holy ones, joined by the Holy Spirit most intimately to the Head, Jesus Christ, continue to share in bringing the healing love of Jesus to the needy and the broken. The saints and the angels have a power, which is Christ's power within them, to intercede, not only for all of us on earth, but in particular for those beings who are in need of healing after their earthly death.

Pray for One Another

One of the most basic beliefs among Christians is that they can pray for one another while on this earth. This belief does not take away from the unique power of Jesus Christ as high priest and intercessor before the heavenly Father but rather is rooted in that very belief. Jesus Christ and his early apostles enjoined the individual Christians and the churches to pray for one another. Basic to this command is the belief that the chosen people of God should pray for the coming of the kingdom, for the well-being of the whole world. Since they were praying in the name of Jesus to the Father, they believed that whatever they asked for in his Spirit would be given. St.

Paul exhorts Timothy: ". . . first of all, there should be prayers offered for everyone—petitions, intercessions and thanksgiving—and especially for kings and others in authority, so that we may be able to live religious and reverent lives in peace and quiet. To do this is right, and will please God our saviour: he wants everybody to be saved and reach full knowledge of the truth" (1 Tm 2:1-4).

St. Clement of Rome exhorts the Corinthian Christians to pray for sinners that they might submit to the divine will. He quotes the example of Esther who prayed to God in fasting and humiliation for her people; God heard her prayer. Therefore, Christians could pray efficaciously for those in sin, "for so shall the compassionate remembrance of them with God and the saints be fruitful unto them and perfect."[2]

This practice of praying for sinners and all persons in need, be it bodily, psychically or spiritually, found its exercises especially in the Eucharistic celebrations. We need only look at the ancient practice so constantly kept alive in the Byzantine Liturgy of St. John Chrysostom of praying for all levels of human beings, those living and those who have passed beyond this earth, the saints and the sinners.

The literature from apostolic times to the present reveals a constant belief in the practice of praying and fasting in intercession for individual persons, churches and all mankind. Out of this continued practice of praying for each other through the intercessory power of Jesus Christ came the starting point for the further development of the doctrine of the communion of saints and all the other related doctrines that somehow or other touch this vital teaching. This basic belief that Christians are able to pray and intercede for one another touches intimately other teachings: the efficacy of prayer, the union between the various states of the church—militant, suffering and triumphant—and the extension of Christ's redemption through the members of his church, his body.

Saints Intercede for the Living

We can safely rely on a unanimous tradition from earliest Christianity that the saints, even after death, remain true members of the kingdom of God. They become even more closely connected with the head in loving and praising the heavenly Father. Moreover, such saints, beginning with the apostles and the martyrs, enjoy a special role of intercession with Christ before the Father. The apostles hold the foremost rank among those who are seated in glory with Jesus Christ. Not only are they singled out for imitation because of their illustrious following of Christ, but they are also considered powerful intercessors on behalf of the faithful on earth.

Innumerable documents can be cited, especially tombstone markings around the burial sites of the first apostles, such as Sts. Peter and Paul in Rome, and the early martyrs, to attest to the belief that the faithful prayed to the great saints who they believed were already in heavenly glory, close to Christ and making intercession on behalf of the living.[3] We find inscriptions written by humble and almost illiterate pilgrims who visited the tombs of the apostles and the martyrs in Rome, Mauretania and Egypt. We find epitaphs in verse about Bishop Abercios of Hieropolis, Pectorius of Autun and Damasus of Rome. Always there is the same confirmation of a common belief and practice in regard to the saints. Pilgrims ask the prayerful intercession of the departed saints who now are in glory through their imitation of Jesus Christ in life and in death. On the tombstones of those who have died are found requests that their fellow Christians, still on earth or the already departed, remember them in prayer.

You can see from so much archeological, literary

and liturgical evidence that the early Christians knew themselves to be a part of a spiritual fraternity, a fellowship which death did not destroy. All had one name, "Christian," and all ate of the same mystical food, the body and blood of Jesus Christ. They worshiped the one God and called upon the one Mediator, Jesus Christ. They honored the same saints, apostles and martyrs and prayed at the shrines where the remains of the saints were venerated, where basilicas and imposing altars were erected.

Such Christians believed that the saints had reached heaven safely while they themselves still pilgrimaged on earth, surrounded by constant dangers and struggles. The angels also had a oneness with such pilgrims and were beseeched for their protection and intercession. All the angels and the saints already glorified in heaven, those departed who still awaited full admission into heaven and those on earth formed one church under the head, Jesus Christ, bonded together by the one common love.

Hippolytus in the third century gives an excellent description of the union of all the elect who share their riches with other Christians, both living and dead.

> What then is the church? The holy assembly of those who live in justice. For concord, which is the way of the saints to fraternity, is the church, the spiritual house of God, founded on Christ in the east, in which all kinds of trees spring up, the generation of the fathers who have been set apart from the beginning, and the works of the prophets perfected according to the law, and the choir of the apostles made wise by the Word, and the martyrs redeemed by Christ's blood, and the vocation of virgins sanctified by water, the choir of teachers and the ordering of bishops,

priests and Levites. All these flourish in the church adorned with all austerity, being unable to decay. Receiving of their fruit, we obtain good understanding, as we eat of the spiritual and heavenly food which grows in them.[4]

Origen, more than any other early writer, formulates in his treatise *On Prayer* the doctrine of the communion of saints. He shows that, if the virtues practiced in this life find in heaven their perfection, then the most perfect of all virtues, that of love for one's neighbor, will be most perfectly exercised in heaven by the saints for those still on earth and for the departed still in need of prayers. He builds his argument on St. Paul's teaching: ". . . that each part may be equally concerned for all the others. If one part is hurt, all parts are hurt with it. If one part is given special honor, all parts enjoy it" (1 Cor 12:25-26). Origen believes that St. Paul's words: ". . . when any man is made to fall, I am tortured" (2 Cor 11:29) can be applied also to the saints who grieve and wish to do all they can to help the weak members of the Body of Christ. Origen appeals to the account in Maccabees where Jeremiah appears and gives Judas Maccabee a golden sword. Onias witnesses to the powerful intercessory prayer of Jeremiah: "This is a man who loves his brothers and prays much for the people and the Holy City— Jeremiah, the prophet of God" (2 Mc 15:14).[5]

Intercession of Angels

Rooted in the Old and New Testaments' doctrine about angels, the early Christian writers regarded the angels as the channels through whom God orders the course of this created world. Part of the work of the angels, therefore, was helping and protecting the faithful in order to lead them into the fullness of redemption and citizenship in the heavenly kingdom. St. Augustine gives a more detailed foundation for belief in the relation between angels and human beings. Angels form the heavenly city of God and this segment of the holy city comes to the help of the other part that is still pilgrimaging below; for both parts will one day be united and even now are one in the bond of love.[6] The angels invite human beings to a share in the kingdom of God and desire that they become citizens.[7] As the angels ministered to Christ, so now they minister to him in heaven and in his body on earth. The angels mount up to the head and descend to the members.[8]

The greater number of both Greek and Latin writers in the early church teaches clearly that each baptized person enjoys the protection and guidance of an individual angel. The Cappadocian Fathers, St. Basil and his brother, St. Gregory of Nyssa and St. John Chrysostom teach clearly that those who believe in Christ and belong to the church have their own individual guardian angels to protect them and urge them on to good works.[9]

What is a consistent doctrine in the church is that God ministers to us on earth and in the life to come through his saints and angels. Such "ministering spirits" (Heb 1:14) are found throughout Holy Scripture as the messengers of God or powers stemming from God. What is important is that they make God's goodness concrete, both in this life and in the life to come. Their manifold ministry to us is considered in scripture and in the writings of the early Fathers as a protection against the dangers which the evil powers place in the way of the faithful. As cities are protected by their walls against the attacks of enemies, so the Christian is protected by the guardian angel.[10]

Angels are described as instructors, leading us on to perform good works.[11] They guide us to eternal blessedness, to the eternal city of God. They bring the prayers of the faithful before God and intercede for those placed under their charge.[12] Billy Graham captures an early patristic teaching in his book on angels when he insists that, as the angels escorted Lazarus to Abraham in heaven, so we shall be escorted by angels into the presence of God upon our deaths.[13]

Just as the veneration of the great saints, the apostles, martyrs and later outstanding confessors, virgins and bishops, led to the building of churches and shrines in their honor, so churches and oratories were constructed to venerate the two princes of the heavenly host, Michael and Gabriel. Such places of veneration in honor of the angels became places of pilgrimage where the afflicted of body and soul came to have their prayers answered through the intercession of the angels. The angels not only found a place in the liturgical calendar, numbered with the saints by special feast days, but the belief and devotion of the faithful in their interceding power and presence were inserted in both liturgies of East and West in the fourth and fifth centuries.

Mary, Queen of Heaven

Although the Virgin Mary, as mother of Jesus and as archetype of the church, had been emphasized by the theologians of the church, especially St. Irenaeus, before the fourth century and the beginning of the Constantinian period, her powerful intercession had not yet received emphasis. With the development of monasticism and the intensification of the ascetical life, Mary becomes the highest ideal of virginity. Another factor that accounts for increased devotion to Mary after the fourth century comes through the development of Christology as the church theologians combatted the various heresies concerning the union of the two natures in one person, Christ. In the East in the Council of Ephesus (431) her title of *Theotokos* (Birthgiver to God, or Mother of God) was fixed for all times as her chief attribute. And from this there stemmed belief in her powerful intercession with her Divine Son to aid the faithful, both in this life and in the life after death.

The devotion of the faithful developed strongly toward Mary, the Mother of God, from the fourth century onward. Of all members of Christ's Body, who but Mary enjoys the highest glory and oneness with Jesus Christ? This reached a peak of devotion that professed, first in the East and then in the West, that Mary received a con-glorification, body, soul and spirit, with Christ in the church's belief in her assumption into heaven. As she intimately shared in the life, suffering and death of her Son, so the church believes Mary shares now in his glory. She served him with the total surrender of herself. She also has come into glory with him. Jesus is the "first fruits and then, after the coming of Christ, those who belong to him" (1 Cor 15:23). Mary belongs most intimately to Jesus as mother to Son, as the living member of his body closest in relation to him, the head.

Too often, devotion to Mary became objectified and rendered static. She was placed in heaven and from time to time asked a favor of her Son on our behalf. Mary's glory, however, like that of Christ, is not a static enjoyment of a heavenly reward. Her glory consists in being present to Jesus Christ and through him present to the heavenly Father by the overshadowing of the Holy Spirit. But being present in love to her Son is to have his very own mind. It is to receive his infinite, perfect gift of himself. But it is also for Mary, along with all the angels and saints, to want continually to surrender herself in loving service.

As Jesus is now interceding for you, so Mary is united with him in seeking to help you. If Mary and the saints, while on earth, lived only for Christ, how much more now does Mary with the saints want to bring all beings to him? This would mean in the teaching of the church that the angels and saints can and do intercede for you when you pray to them. It means that Mary and the angels and saints are now living with full consciousness, memory and understanding of our needs, of the needs of all the living on earth and those who have passed into the future life. She, above all the angels and other saints, exercises acts of love and compassion toward all of us, especially toward the most needy.

Can you believe that Mary, who loved Jesus Christ so ardently in her lifetime, does not now burn with love and zeal to share her Son with all of us? If St. Paul yearned with great zeal to become all things to all men in order to win them for Christ (1 Cor 9:22), you can imagine the interest and zeal of Mary and the other great saints in regard to all human beings, including those who have already died. St. Paul felt a spiritual maternity toward those whom he formed. "I must go through the pain of giving birth to you all over again, until Christ is formed in you" (Gal 4:19). Mary, who in her earthly life gave birth to Christ wants continually in her glory to form Christ in all the children he has given her.

An Active Presence to Us

The church has always taught doctrinally and devotionally that there is communication between the living in this life and those living in Christ in the life after death. Vatican II's *Constitution on the Church* reiterates this constant tradition: "The church too has devoutly implored the aid of their (those living the life in Christ after death) intercession." [14] St. John of the Cross highlights how love limits the body: "The soul lives where it loves rather than in the body which it animates, because it has not its life in the body, but rather gives it to the body and lives through love in that which it loves."[15]

We implore the intercession of the dead because we believe they are even more alive and more loving, hence more desirous of helping us, than when they lived their earthly life. Those who die are as real as the love relationships formed in this life. Their limitations, and their degree of reality, are fashioned, not by a material localization, but by God's power of love within them. Faith among Christians down through the centuries insures us that we can be in spiritual communion with the angels and saints, as well as our loved ones, relatives and friends who have passed through death into eternal life.

Among all Christians departed into life eternal, Mary is the most "possessed" by God's spirit of love; the most "full of grace." She is "higher in honor than the cherubim and more glorious beyond compare than the seraphim," as the Byzantine Liturgy of St. John Chrysostom hymns her. She is more present to us than our most beloved parents, husband or wife or friends departed.

She is present to us by the immense "oneness" that she enjoys with the "oneness" of the Trinity. The prayer of Jesus to his Father in the Last Supper Discourse was fulfilled for his mother, at least:

> Father, may they be one in us,
> As you are in me and I am in you. . .
> With me in them and you in me,
> may they be so completely one. . .
> I want those you have given me
> to be with me where I am,
> so that they may always see the glory
> you have given me. . . (Jn 17:21-24).

But Mary is also present universally to every human being by her activating love that seeks to serve the neediest of the children whom she ardently wishes to bring forth into God's life. At the heart of Mary's love and our love is a desire to share abundantly with others who do not have what we have, the goodness God has given us.

The greater the gifts of love that you receive, the more you have to share with others. Upon entering into her glory in heaven, Mary was full of grace. She was already declared full of grace by the angel Gabriel when the Holy Spirit overshadowed her and she surrendered completely to serve her Lord in her humble lowliness (Lk 1:38). Yet she grew in love of God as she allowed God's love in her to make her more open, more present, more serving to all who needed her. How she must have grown in grace as she served her Son Jesus at Nazareth for 30 years! At the foot of the cross, how that grace must have reached a fullness that pained her to want to be present to each person in the whole world in order that the blood of her Son and God might not be poured out in vain!

The Saints Grow by Loving Service

Think of Mary and the great saints who have come into full existence in Christ by serving the Body of Christ! How she and they must have grown in greater grace, in greater presence of God-in-them, as love, toward the whole world! In a way, Mary and the angels and saints, even our loved ones who have left this earth, need us so that they may exercise God's immense love burning within them by letting it out in loving service to the needy ones, both to those in this earthly existence and to those who are in need of healing therapy in the condition in which they find themselves after their death. Like a mother who needs a sick or retarded child to allow her the occasion and the conflict necessary for her to grow in greater self-giving love, so Mary and the saints and angels need the sinful and ignorant who live in darkness and absence of their Lord and Savior. With Christ living in them, they lovingly intercede for the needy as only a suffering mother can: "Father, forgive them, they do not know what they are doing" (Lk 23:34). Unlike the most needy on earth and in the life to come, the advanced contemplatives are those with whom Mary and the great ones in heaven can share their contemplative insights. Even the ordinary Christian, no great sinner or saint, calls out a unique form of service from Mary, the angels and the other saints, who urge him to greater love through their exercise of a loving service to other members of the Body of Christ.

Suffering with Christ

How can the saints along with Mary be in glory and still able to show compassion toward the broken and the needy and even suffer with them? How do your coldnesses, tepidity and sinfulness affect the saints in glory? Vatican II declared that the saints are in glory along with Mary. This would mean that they have been glorified, not only in their souls, but as total persons along with all their experiences acquired in earthly living. The saints can relive their suffering moments as they now apply such knowledge to new experiences in relationships with new events and persons who, both in their earthly existence or in life after death, present themselves as actual or potential members of the same Body of Christ of which the saints are such outstanding members.

How can a loving involvement with someone in great physical, psychic or spiritual suffering not bring some share of suffering to the empathetic one who suffers to do more to alleviate such pain? Can Mary and the angels and saints be in touch with each period of history in general and with the specific history of individual persons that they are drawn by grace to help and not somehow or other suffer also? Their joy is full in their union with Christ and with the other saints. Their joyful, loving service admits to pain in their partial union with those undergoing the healing therapy of purgatory. Their pain becomes a sharing in the agonizing, excruciating pain of those who find themselves in the throes of the condition called hell. They fill up the sufferings in the Body of Christ by such loving service. They enter into the role of victim-priest that Jesus Christ enjoys, a role he shares with the healthy members of his Body in the life to come, just as he shares it with the living saints on earth.

Origen describes the filling up of the sufferings of Christ as Christ remaining on the cross as long as one sinner remains in hell. [16] If the saints are tied not only to the loved ones whom they came to know while on earth but also to the many brothers and sisters, fellow members of the Body of Christ whom they have not yet met personally except through Jesus Christ, their head, would it be beyond our Christian faith to believe that such saints do have a loving and a suffering concern for us in our many needs, for all of us, on earth and in purgatory and in hell? They know the Lord now, not by faith but "face to face." Yet do they not know also the Lord's face in the actual or potential members of his very body as they suffer to see them in their great need of knowledge and love of Jesus Christ?

A Healing Society

We have pointed out how persons in the state of purgatory or hell cannot heal themselves merely by wanting to do so, but depend on other healthy members to love them into new being and bring the healing, compassionate merciful love of God to them. As I grow older in my priestly ministry, I become more compassionate toward sinners who come to be healed in the sacrament of reconciliation. I begin to see the awfulness of sin as a darkening of man's ability to see God. One individual's view is darkened because he was forced to grow up in a broken family and at an early age was on the streets in gangs who knew only violence and hatred for the moneyed classes; another was spoiled by wealthy parents and never knew self-discipline, but only self-indulgence; yet another was fed an Irish Jansenism that feared sex. I ask how much their brokenness was a deliberate act of turning away from God and how much it was the responsibility of their society. The evident truth is that here are broken people who need the healing love of Jesus Christ.

When I ponder the power of culture to keep a whole nation tied to a religion that militates against Christianity or that has experienced, as a colony of so-called Christian colonial nations, Christianity as a religion of the "ruling" and exploiting class, then I ask: "Lord, what about the billions in history who through society's limitations never had a chance truly to know you?"

If society and groups of individuals are so powerful in shaping the acts and values of human beings for all eternity, would not God in his mercy allow a new society, his church triumphant, to be the means to reveal his compassion for them and lead them from the level of love that they attained during their lives to new levels of loving union with others? We have seen that human beings die and bring with them into eternity that level of consciousness which they had reached during their human existence by making choices in accord with their consciences. If the church's doctrine about purgatory had any truth to it, it would mean that a therapy is at work in the life to come for those who have not totally separated themselves from God.

Can you not believe that the saints and even your loved ones who are still attached to you by so many bonds of human love, even though they have entered into their purification process before you, not only will help you, but in a real way they need you in order to allow their great love for God to unfold and be actualized in a new, expanded consciousness? They are like those who have graduated with advanced degrees and are teaching you on this earth, or in the state of healing therapy in life after death, how to read, write and do simple problems in the spiritual life. All who believe in Jesus Christ are living members of his body and this presence to each member transcends the temporal and spatial limitations of their imperfect existence on this earth. Milton expresses this belief: "Millions of spiritual creatures walk the earth unseen, both when we wake and when we sleep."[17]

The following is an imagined vision of the way I conceive the life to come, drawing upon the insights that have been gathered from Holy Scripture and church tradition. Would it be too farfetched to imagine that, similar to this life's existence, so in the life to come there is some interaction between persons in their new spiritualized existence? Is this not what the church has been teaching us for 2,000 years, namely, that you can pray to the saints and they can know what you are asking and, therefore, they can offer your prayers to Jesus Christ and the heavenly Father? If the saints and angels—because of their fullness of grace and their closeness in the Body of Christ to the head, Jesus—can be in communication with you, could you not also think that your human love for your friends will be the means of mutual communication?

In a third-century epitaph we find this type of belief expressed by a certain Pectorius who had it carved over his tomb:

> O Fish, feed then thine own, I beseech thee,
>   Lord Redeemer.
> May my mother rest here in peace, I implore thee,
>   Light of the dead.
> Aschandus, O Father, very dear to my heart, as
>   you remember my sweet
> mother and my brothers

In the peace of the Fish, remember thy Pectorius.[18]

Pectorius prays to the Lord for the repose of his mother and he begs his father Aschandus not to forget him in his prayer to Christ any more than he forgets his wife and his other children.

Someday we will understand how our loved ones, along with the angels and our favorite saints, were most influential in helping us to love God while we were on this earth. How sad it is that Christians, even if they do intellectually accept the fact that angels and saints can intercede for them, do not daily live out this belief. This applies to so many Christians who seemingly forget to remember their loved ones, both to pray for them, and especially to let them know of their earthly needs. Although your loved ones may not rival in holiness the great saints, still they are quite closely tied to you by God's gifting you with their love. The power of God still works in them, giving them a loyalty to you that impels them to help you with your every need, just as they wanted to do, while they lived on this earth.

If you take this ancient doctrine of the communion of saints seriously, you should be able to walk and talk with your departed loved ones. The love of God in them that still binds them closely to you becomes the powerful "wavelength" by which they can communicate with you. The greater your love for them, the greater the communication. You cannot communicate with a nonentity; there must be knowledge of the existence of such an intellectual being. Then there must be discourse leading to loving union or communion. If you believe that the dead are in the Body of Christ, having lived in this existence and having died in Jesus Christ, and you equally believe, by God's grace, that you also are in the same Body of Christ, then it means that you are intimately united with them.

The level of love that the departed have attained in loving us in this life cannot remain on a static level but needs to expand through loving concern and humble service for the ones loved. They need to exercise their love for us and this they do in many ways that would include all of the ways by which they wished to show their love for us while they were on this earth. We have helped them become what they are in the Body of Christ by our returned love to them. They now realize how intimately we are a part of their existence and their love for God. Their charity begins closest to the community that surrounds them and we are most intimately tied by God's providence to their core of being. Thus they can be powerful aids to come to our assistance with their purified love for us and their new knowledge of their relationship along with ours to the whole Body of Christ.

Without making a judgment on the holiness of such a servant of God as Kathryn Kuhlman, would it be far-fetched that God, who surely used her to touch millions of lives in her ministry of healing while she lived on earth, would also use her and so many other powerful healers, if we were to ask their intercession? This we Catholics can easily accept in the case of the great saints who have had their miracles and healings confirmed by the church. But the beautiful doctrine of the intercession of the saints is that all who are in the Body of Christ are united with the head, Jesus Christ, and enjoy the privilege but also the duty to build up the members in the body. If we, to use St. Paul's analogy of the human body to describe the Mystical Body of Christ, are simple parts, doing our little bit in the whole body, the church, would it not follow that other simple persons, who have already passed into life eternal and have died in Christ, could be very close to us in relationship to time in history, nationality, church membership, bonds of marriage, bloodlines or merely an attraction in grace given us toward such a "little saint"?

Zeal to Help Others

If we love one another, then God's love is being perfected in us (1 Jn 4:12). Many of the saints have expressed this belief that in the life to come they wish to spend themselves helping persons still living on this earth. St. Dominic, founder of the Dominican Order, promised his confreres that he would be more useful to them after his death than while he was still living. St. Therese of Lisieux wanted to remain seated at the table of sinners in her solidarity with them. She promised to help her missionary friends more in heaven than she did through her prayers and sacrifices while on earth. The sacrifice of oneself in place of others is at the heart of Christianity. "A man can have no greater love than to lay down his life for his friends," said Jesus (Jn 15:13). As he died on the cross in imitation of the self-emptying love of his heavenly Father toward each of his children, so his Holy Spirit inspires his disciples that the only sign whereby people will recognize them as his followers is by the love they have for one another, for all persons.

I like to think (and how this will be done remains a mystery only for us who are still on this earth) that the mercy and love of God, Father, Son and Holy Spirit, continually go out in uncreated energies of love toward every human and angelic being created by God for union in the Body of Christ. God's healing love surely never ceases to pursue his children, especially those who have the greatest need. If so many billions and billions of human beings have never known his immense love for mankind in Christ Jesus, so often through no fault of their own, does not God continue to bring his healing love to such through the announcing of the Good News by those who are the healthy members of the Body of Christ? I like to believe that Jesus walks among such broken ones who have passed into eternal life, even as he walks in this earthly economy of salvation, through the loving eyes, hands, lips of those who have been privileged to know Jesus Christ as their personal Savior. I like to imagine that the quivering lips of frightened children will be soothed to a smile, hatred of killers and prejudices of non-Christians toward Christ and his followers will be dissolved by loving persons ready to do all to help the others become fully realized persons. "But why are you so loving? Who are you? What have I ever done for you?" Then the followers of Jesus will finally understand his words: "I tell you solemnly, in so far as you did this to one of the least of these brothers of mine, you did it to me" (Mt 25:40). And the broken ones will experience Jesus touching them and bringing them into fullness of life. Those who never knew Jesus Christ will be led to the head through his members, as they joyfully confess: "We never knew such love!"

The Coming of Christ

We believe that Christ will come at the end of time in the *Parousia*, the appearance of Christ in glory, to transform this universe by bringing it to its completion in and through himself. But in a real sense, the *Parousia* is already present in our universe for persons of deep prayer. For them, through faith, hope and love in Jesus Christ, the master is always coming in his glorified saints and angels. By their union with him, he is now achieving the victory over cosmic evil through all of his members on earth and those living in him in eternal life.

He is precisely overcoming the forces of death, sin and chaos and is bringing about a gradual transfiguration of the entire creation of God, fashioning it through his members into the fullness of his very own resurrection body, the church. But this transfiguration process, since it is energized by God's very own uncreated energies of love living inside his alive members, will stretch forth, always resting in the freshness of the love acquired and enjoyed in contemplation; yet always restless to love more by serving those who are in great need of his love. The greater the saint is in holiness and the closer such a one comes to the head that is Christ, the more that saint wishes to serve in humble love.

St. Paul applied the following words to those living still on this earth, but how fitting a conclusion to this chapter on communion with the saints to apply them to those who die in Christ and live eternally to love others into new life in him. This is reconciliation. This is the gathering of all created beings into the firstborn, Jesus Christ (Col 1:15).

> And for anyone who is in Christ, there is a new creation; the old creation has gone, and now the new one is here. It is all God's work. It was God who reconciled us to himself through Christ and gave us the work of handing on this reconciliation. In other words, God in Christ was reconciling the world to himself, not holding men's faults against them, and he has entrusted to us the news that they are reconciled. So we are ambassadors for Christ; it is as though God were appealing through us, and the appeal that we make in Christ's name is: be reconciled to God. For our sake God made the Sinless One into sin, so that in him we might become the goodness of God (2 Cor 5:17-21).

The greatest creative power in all the universe is to forget oneself in order unselfishly to love another into being. The saints are God's successful children, oriented outward to bring God's love to all they meet. They live in the experiential contemplation of the trinitarian community, Father begetting them as his children in his Son,

Jesus, through the Spirit of love. Such unique identity in Christ allows them to spend themselves in loving self-sacrifice by the power of the indwelling Trinity, transforming them into diaphanous, luminous icons of God's unique love for every created angel and saint.

Heaven, ultimately, is God, ever evolving more and more into Love, made manifest in Christ Jesus by the love of God in his angels and saints, allowing them with God's energy to love and serve others and thus bring all creation into the Body of Christ. Heaven, through the loving communion of the angels and saints, is the state of realization that: "There is only Christ; he is everything and he is in everything" (Col 3:11).

Chapter Seven
He Descended into Hell

The Christian life as taught and lived by Jesus Christ is rooted in the very nature of the triune God. God is love, always loving by nature. If he could not love he would cease to be God. His love is active, surrounding and permeating us. His love is not limited by time or space. He knows only a presence that is self-giving toward union.

The manner in which Western Christians—Roman Catholics and Protestants—have interpreted and preached the doctrine of hell horrendously distorts this vision of a gentle, loving God. This doctrine puts an *animus* vindictiveness into God that all too often constitutes a great and sad superstition. If you wish to test an individual Christian's life, ask what he or she believes about hell. I mean really believes! For like all other dogmas and doctrines, we can give an intellectual assent to what we think hell is like, but we may, fortunately, not live by its awful consequences. We may truly believe, somehow or other, in mystery, that God's love and mercy are greater than his zeal for vindictive punishment for all eternity.

No doctrine taught by Christian Churches has been

so misunderstood as the past and present teachings con--
cerning hell, at least among Western Christians. The root
of the problem lies in our penchant for objectification.
When theology became a speculative science separated
from mystery and mysticism, our theologians yielded to
the temptation, described by Louvain philosopher G.
Philips, as "the widespread habit of speaking of God and
divine realities and of reducing faith to a string of
speculative propositions."[1]

Our preachers, following the teaching on hell offered
by the theologians, had a great, psychological "hammer"
with which to pound their listeners into fearful submission. They preached about a lurid place into which God
in his righteous wrath hurls millions of souls. There they
are tormented by the worm of conscience, physical fires,
sulphur and brimstone. Amid such terrifying and unending sufferings somehow or other God and his saved
"saints" rejoice to see that justice is being done and the
unjust are finally receiving their due.

In the third century Tertullian projected something of
his own disturbed *animus* into the teaching on hell that
has never quite been absent in the West:

> At that greatest of all spectacles, the last and
> eternal judgment, how shall I admire, how
> laugh, how rejoice, how exult, when I behold
> so many proud monarchs groaning in the
> lowest abyss of darkness; so many
> magistrates liquefying in fiercer flames than
> they ever kindled against the Christians; so
> many sage philosophers blushing in red-hot
> fires with their deluded pupils; so many trage-
> dians more tuneful in the expression of their
> own sufferings; so many dancers tripping
> more nimbly from anguish than ever before
> from applause.[2]

We know Jesus preached a hell of fire and punishment. He used the imagery prevalent among the Jews of his day to describe the existence of hell as a place of eternal fire. He was a preacher; he was also divine. Although he described hell in words and images that came from Persian and Jewish apocalyptic literature current in his day, especially as taught by the leading Pharisees, he was saying something that went far beyond the literalness of such images that can be found in nearly all religions.

Hindu and Persian writings present a hell in imagery similar to what Jesus used and what was popularly known to his listeners. Yet we can hardly believe that such pre-Christian descriptions of the anguishes of hell, of eternally raging furnaces, are truly divine revelation. Hesiod, Homer and Virgil give us previews of the subterranean levels of hell that surely must have had an influence upon Jewish and Christian descriptions of the eternal punishments that await the sinful.

What did Jesus mean when he used such popular, metaphorical language? He was speaking to the conscience of his listeners and was leading them into a mystery, not a literal preview, of what follows their choices in this life. But Christian theologians and preachers have taken his imagery, popularly drawn in the Judaism of his day and from pagan sources, and taught a hell that has made a mockery of the rest of Jesus' teaching and of his very person.

St. Augustine argues philosophically to show how the material bodies of the damned will not be annihilated but will burn in everlasting, material fire.[3] St. Thomas Aquinas believed that for God and the saints in heaven part of their celestial happiness consisted in viewing the terrifying punishments endured eternally by the damned. "That the saints may enjoy their beatitude and the grace of God more richly, a perfect sight of the punishment of the damned is granted to them."[4]

Human vindictiveness seems to fashion such a trait and attribute it to God, but surely not the God that Jesus revealed to us. An example of this is the description of hell given by Jonathan Edwards, an 18th-century American Protestant divine, who thought he was doing nothing but commenting on Jesus' own words:

> The world will probably be converted into a great lake or liquid globe of fire, a vast ocean of fire, in which the wicked shall be over-whelmed, which will always be in tempest, in which they shall be tossed to and fro, having no rest day or night, vast waves or billows of fire continually rolling over their heads, of which they shall forever be full of a quick sense within and without: their heads, their eyes, their tongues, their hands, their feet, their loins, and their vitals shall forever be full of a glowing, melting fire, fierce enough to melt the very rocks and elements; and also they shall eternally be full of the most quick, and lively sense to feel the torments; not for one minute, nor for one day, nor for one age, nor for two ages, nor for a hundred ages, nor for ten thousands of millions of ages one after another, but for ever and ever, without any end at all, and never, never be delivered.[5]

How can such a vindictive God be the same merciful and forgiving God who can never be but eternally and unchangingly a loving father? If God so loved the world and wished each individual to share his life when he gave us his Son who died that we might have eternal life (Jn 3:16), then how can that God build a fiery hell and punish millions for all eternity and rejoice that his justice is being accomplished?

A Reinterpretation

Fortunately, today many biblical scholars and theologians are taking a new look at the church's doctrine of hell. Through contact with other non-Christian religions and their sacred books, along with scholarly work done concerning Egyptian, Persian and Greek influences upon the intertestamental apocryphal works of Judaism, such as the book of Enoch (written about 200 B.C.), these scholars show us how the popular imagery and language current at the time that our Lord preached about hell depended on such sources.

Also, as we learn more about human psychology, we see how our present choices and human relationships shape us, both in this life and surely in the life to come, to be the persons we now are and will be after death. It becomes much easier in our modern world to believe that God does not create a "place" where he punishes us with material fire, but that the meaning which Jesus meant to convey was even greater self-punishment from within, according to our own human choices.

God does not send us to hell. If we continue to make choices based on selfishness rather than self-sacrificing love, we will evolve to a state of "aloneness," a state that is destruction of God's true life shared through authentic love of others. Hell must be found in man's heart and not in some "place" below the earth. God can never go against his nature to always love us, yet we can continuously make choices that form a state of consciousness that separates us from God and our world.

Ladislaus Boros is typical of the modern, insightful theologian who offers us a new way of viewing the traditional doctrine of hell. Such a theologian does not wish to discard, but to highlight more the true message of Christ about the awfulness of hell. He writes:

> Hell is not something that simply happens
> from outside; it is not something that God im-
> poses on us afterwards for our misdeeds. . . .
> It is the mode of existence of a human being
> who is satisfied in himself, for all eternity; he
> has nothing more and desires nothing more
> than himself. . . . There is no tragic grandeur
> about hell, because fundamentally there can
> not be any "place" which is hell. There is only
> a state of heart.[6]

The existence of hell for such theologians is not
denied but rather is made even more real than for those
who in earlier times accepted literally the images of
banishment from God that were so heavily bathed in
physical pain. As such, hell becomes a symbol of a state
of existence that Jesus is warning us about. Hell begins
when any human sets up a pattern of self-centered living
and is outside God's loving communication. Such an
understanding of hell does not allow one to objectify a
future punishment, but it forces a decision at each moment to freely choose alienation from God or from one's
false self.

C.S. Lewis, in *The Great Divorce*, describes hell as a
grey town in which the inhabitants cannot get along.
They keep moving farther and farther away from one
another and from the bus station in the center of town
that could take them to the outskirts of heaven. They
refuse to leave their state of alienation from God and
others. Hell for Lewis is a picture of individuals frantically
trying not to be neighbors because of self-centered habits
that first began on earth.[7]

Revealed Truths

As a Christian, you must be guided by God's revelation. Just what do you learn of the doctrine of hell from
Holy Scripture? And can you accept as literal the words

used without studying their context and the intended meaning of the authors?

Earlier I pointed out the gradual evolution of the early Judaic concept of *Sheol*. It was first seen as a subterranean hollow which received all the dead equally. It was a land of gloom and darkness, a state of dreamy half-existence. Under the influence of Persian and the Jewish apocalyptic literature in the second and first centuries before Christ, the concept of Sheol (or Hades in Greek) underwent a change.

Under the influences of the doctrines of the immortality of the soul and resurrection, Sheol or Hades was divided into two distinct parts. The upper part was reserved for the righteous who awaited the final resurrection while the lower, called *Gehenna*, received the wicked who were tormented with terrifying punishments. In the apocalyptic Book of Enoch, which was highly influenced by Persian eschatology, we find such vivid imagery of hell as a place of punishment through material fire, worms, ice, cold, chains, brimstone, sulphur and darkness.

Although writings of the Septuagint (such as the Book of Daniel and the second Book of Maccabees) use words as "eternal" and "everlasting" (*aionios* in Greek), the meaning is a popular description for an indefinite duration of a long period of time. But in no way did the writers mean it to be a metaphysical concept of unending, everlasting timelessness as we understand it today.

In the New Testament we have a similar doctrine taught, even through the words attributed to Jesus by the synoptic writers of the Gospels, of a place of everlasting punishment by unquenchable fire. Scripture scholar J.L. McKenzie brings together the New Testament references to hell.[8] Gehenna or hell is mentioned seven times in the Gospel of Matthew; three times in Mark, once in Luke and once in St. James' Epistle. It is described in imagery commonly accepted among the contemporaries of Jesus as a place of fire (Mt 5:22), of unquenchable fire (Mk 9:43); and a place where the wicked are destroyed, both in body and soul (Mt 10:28; Lk 12:5).

Hell is a "place" of punishment, a prison and torture chamber (Mt 5:25-26). There will be "weeping and grinding of teeth" (Mt 8:12). In hell the worm does not die (Mk 9:48) since it is an everlasting punishment (Mt 25:46). Most of these statements are attributed to Jesus, but can we ever be sure that they are his actual words or the words of the evangelists summing up his teaching?[9]

Jewish apocalyptic imagery is found abundantly in the Book of Revelation, attributed to St. John the Evangelist, especially in the following statement: "Then the devil, who misled them, will be thrown into a lake of fire and sulphur, where the beast and the false prophet are, and their torture will not stop, day or night, for ever and ever" (Rv 20:10; also Rv 21:8; Jude 6-7). Are you to take such imagery as a true objective presentation by Christ and the early church concerning hell?

McKenzie gives us the thinking of modern, biblical scholars:

> Comparison of these New Testament passages with the passages of the apocryphal books cited above shows that the Synoptic Gospels, Jude, Jm, 2P and Rv employ the language and imagery of contemporary Judaism. It is remarkable that this language and imagery do not appear in other New Testament writings. These passages suggest that the apocalyptic imagery. . . is to be taken for what it is, imagery, and not as strictly literal theological affirmations.[10]

From the language found in the New Testament it is

clearly taught that such a state of separation exists between God and any human being who persists in rejecting God as supreme in his life. It is described in Jewish imagery as an enduring punishment, a state of hopeless and complete frustration, a stranger to the saints and God. We cannot, therefore, by mere reading of scripture, come to a clear and objective concept of hell. Karl Rahner insists that "the metaphors in which Jesus describes the eternal perdition of man as a possibility which threatens him at this moment are images (fire, worm, darkness) taken from the mental furniture of contemporary apocalyptic literature. . . . Even such a term as 'eternal loss' is in the nature of an image."[11]

Church Teaching on Hell

The church guides us in the right doctrine and the right interpretation of scripture through its unerring "consensus ecclesiae" that presents a rather well-defined and consistent doctrine on hell. But even such teaching and documents from church councils need to be studied in the light of the historical context to see exactly what the church was saying in the light of some erroneous doctrine. Theologian Bernard Lonergan makes this point clear when he writes: "The dogmas are permanent in their meaning. . . . What permanently is true, is the meaning of the dogma in the context in which it was defined."[12]

There seems little dispute that the church teaches the definitive existence of hell. We find, however, difficulties in interpreting the scriptural imagery in regard to the eternity of hell and the nature of its punishment. A summation of church teaching as found in its documents throughout history is given us by Karl Rahner:

> In its official teaching the Church has defined the existence of hell (DS

72,76,801,858,1306) and its eternity against the doctrine of the apocatastasis as put forward by Origen and other ancient writers (DS 411). The Church affirmed that entry into hell takes place immediately after their death (DS 858,1002), and made a certain distinction between the loss of the vision of God *(poena damni)* and the pain of sense *(poena sensus)* (DS 780), but apart from this there is no official declaration on the nature of the pains of hell, though the difference of punishments in hell is mentioned (DS 858,1306).[13]

The church has always been vigilant to avoid teaching or encouraging any tendency toward universalism (all humans will eventually be saved) and annihilationism (at the end of time all souls in hell will be destroyed). Universalism appears periodically throughout church history, beginning when teachers, following Origen, the first great biblical exegete, emphasized the overwhelming love and mercy of God. Such a teaching holds that God will continue to extend an opportunity for those in hell to eventually win heaven. Hell, therefore, is not eternal in this teaching and will be dissolved when every human and angelic being is given enough opportunities to win heaven.[14]

There are many conciliar documents that deny universalism and insist on everlasting punishment in hell. The councils of Florence, Lateran IV, Trent and the dogmatic creed, the *Quicunque,* all speak of everlasting fire in hell and perpetual punishment for the wicked sentenced to hell.[15] But again we come back to the problem of whether such council fathers were not battling the doctrine of universalism and employed the scriptural language of everlasting punishment to teach that there is no way out of hell.

Annihilationism maintains that those in hell after the final judgment will be destroyed or annihilated and only those who enjoy eternal life in Christ will live forever. Its adherents base their arguments on an interpretation of texts found in the writings of St. Paul who said that immortality is dependent on being united with Christ (Rom 8:11) and that the wicked ultimately will be annihilated because they will receive "destruction" and "ruin" (1 Tm 6:9; Rom 9:22; Phil 3:19).

A typical explanation by one who holds this doctrine is given by Arthur Chambers, a 19th-century Episcopal writer:

> Following this hell will be another and final experience, "the Second Death," in which those unconnected with Christ, "the Life," will *pass out of existence.* The disease of sin unchecked and uncured by the great physician will have done, as all unchecked disease does; it will have worked out its course to dissolution. The man will die, body and soul, in that second death, because he will be incapable of living. He has not come to Christ that he "might have life" (Jn 5:40).[16]

Such a doctrine, even though it is still taught today among Mormons and Jehovah's Witnesses, is not supported by scripture or the universal teaching of Christianity.[17] For 2,000 years the church has interpreted the Last Judgment discourse as a clear indication in the teaching of Jesus that the condemned will not be destroyed but "will go away to eternal punishment" (Mt 25:46).

A New Look at Hell

Dogma and tradition show a dialectic between the original truth and the interpretation given by the church at any given time in history. Any church interpretation of the teachings on hell is necessarily immersed heavily in encrustations of cultural imagery and problems that arose in Christian times and that seemingly threatened the core of truth always held by the church.

This is why theologians today are seeking a new look at hell. Yet realistically no one can examine such a doctrine of hell without realizing that the past traditions still exercise an important influence on one's present-day thinking. Karl Rahner calls for a "hermeneutics" on the hermeneutics, as found in scripture and the church's traditional, although evolving, teaching on eschatology.[18]

Especially concerning the doctrine of hell, modern theologians are seeking a new understanding that will, hopefully, not lose or destroy the truly revealed elements of this doctrine, but rather will highlight Christ's essential teaching. Our modern age, as the Holy Spirit so clearly indicates through Vatican II, puts great emphasis on our continued growth through freely choosing to participate in the creative development of God's world. The future is no static container already fixed and waiting for us. On the contrary, we and God are now, at this moment, creating our world. The present moment is all-important. In fact, it is all that we have to work on.

In such a vision we moderns can readily see that hell is not so much a future "thing," a place created by God to punish the wicked. Rather, it becomes a most important consideration, as Jesus surely insisted upon when he spoke about hell, about how we are now to live. Hell is about the life to come but it must be seen also as a state or condition of existence that grows out of our moral decisions made in this earthly existence.[19]

Jesus and the church's interpretation of his teaching on hell have stressed the ultimate accountability to ourselves for the way in which we now live our lives. This central truth in times past all too often was not brought into prime focus but buried amid the lurid details of what punishments awaited eternally those who were sentenced to hell.

It is within your power to create the conditions, even now, in which you will live forever in the life to come. Freedom is what makes you human. It also makes hell a real possibility, if you habitually choose in this life to act in a self-centered way. This concept is well expressed by author Patrick Fannon:

> Hell must be understood as a symbol for the eternal possibility of man's present and future existence. Even now hell is experienced as present in the torment and suffering of a man's experience of failure or inability to love God, man, or even himself. Hell is not a place. Nor is it an eternal destiny running parallel to heaven. . . hell is simply destruction and death, the failure to enter into eternity, into the eternal life of God.[20]

The Problem of Hell

You can readily understand that in the life to come you are the sum of relationships that you have freely entered into while on this earth. Unselfish love toward others or self-centeredness will determine whether you will relate in the life to come to God, the world and others in self-sacrificing love or in selfishness. The crucial problem of hell revolves around our return to the fundamental vision of God as a loving Father whose love endures forever. God's uncreated energies of love are relational to all human and angelic beings and never can be controlled by the conditions of earthly space and time. How can Holy Scripture present such a loving, merciful God, along with the scriptural vision of God bringing about all things in fulfillment through his Son Jesus Christ, and still allow for individual human and angelic spirits to be condemned in eternal punishment?

Is it possible for a human to overcome the evil habits of selfishness contracted in this life when he or she reaches the state of hell?

Can you really ask the question whether there are persons suffering eternally in hell? Does the mystery of God's merciful love and man's free will submit to human objectification? To approach this problem let us heed the caution given by C.S. Lewis:

> All answers deceive. If you put the question (whether, as Paul seems to say that all men will be saved) from within time and are asking about possibility the answer is certain. The choice of ways is before you. Neither is closed. Any man may choose eternal death. But if you are trying to leap on into eternity, if you are trying to see the final state of all things as it will be when there are no possibilities left, but only the Real, then you ask what cannot be answered to mortal ears. Time is the very lens through which you see, small and clear, as men see through the wrong end of a telescope, something that would otherwise be too big for you to see at all.[21]

Origen and St. Gregory of Nyssa both grappled with this basic problem of hell and the seeming struggle to pit God's omnipotence and love against man's free will. As with scripture and the church's teaching, they both taught that hell, as a condition of rebellion from God, can exist and have eternal qualities. But eternity is not to be measured in terms of our historical experience. In their teaching on *apokatastasis* or the eventual return of all beings to the loving embrace of God, they insisted on the elements of scripture that present a universal recapitulation process through Christ in which all beings will be won to God.

All Things Subject to God

St. Paul especially insists on the resurrectional power of Christ to recreate *all* men. "And when everything is subjected to him, then the Son himself will be subject in his turn to the One who subjected all things to him, so that God may be all in all" (1 Cor 15:28). Again in his letter to the Ephesians, Paul maintains that: "He has put all things under his feet and made him, as the ruler of everything, the head of the church; which is his body, the fullness of him who fills the whole creation" (Eph 1:22-23). And in Rom 5:18, he claims: "Again, as one man's fall brought condemnation on everyone, so the good act of one man brings everyone life and makes them justified."

The constant picture given us by Jesus of our heavenly Father who loves us with an everlasting love confirms these texts. If God's love is constant and unchanging, even before the awesome prospect of hell, which is to say, before the terrifying possibility of puny man saying no to an infinite love of God manifested to us in his Son dying for love of us, then from God's viewpoint there is always an open channel of his self-giving to all mankind.

In contrast to this general view from God's vantage, we find the other view of a world divided into sheep and goats, the saved and the damned, heaven and hell. This hell is everlasting fire as the text of Mt 25 pictures it.

Can these two views be reconciled? As long as we project our vision of *chronos,* our human objectification of chronological time, upon this problem, the choice before man is an either/or. For man choosing, salvation is truly either God or no God; either a choice of love and happiness with God and in God or an infinitely, everlasting fire of human frustration. But as Emil Brunner points out in his short work, *The Divine-Human En-*

counter,[22] we create a theological shipwreck by reducing to objective concepts that which is so personal and unique that it can be discovered only in the intimacy of a love experience with a *Thou*. Why must human freedom be objectified so that it becomes opposed to the omnipotence of God? We should, however, learn to see freedom as a privilege, an opening to new complexity, a greater richness in being—a movement toward realizing by intersubjective possession that which our whole being yearns for.

But can a person in hell be free and God be omnipotent and still both be reconciled? It is here that we must refuse with Christ (and the wisdom of the church that has never defined that any one concrete being is in hell) to answer this question posed in Lk 13:23: "Sir, will there be only a few saved?" Jesus replied only: "Try your best to enter by the narrow door." For man making the great decision and for Christ and for every teacher concerned with exhorting man in this life to choose rightly, hell is possible. It is in a very real sense eternal. There is something as real in the terrifying punishment as everlasting fire. It is irreversible. It is beyond man's freedom to change his decision. He can choose in this earthly life and his choice, as far as his human powers go to change it, is irrevocable. Hell is a most real possibility as a human being makes his choices in this life, and it is everlasting frustration.

An Everlasting Love

From Christ's side, there is another perspective that is of a totally different nature. Man cannot alter his eternal loss. He can only exist in an everlasting pain of being deprived of God. But the Gospel message tells us that God wants and wills that all men be saved (1 Tm 2:5; Jn 3:16-17). For God to will the salvation of all men is for God continuously to love each person in a unique, personal, self-involving encounter.

What is humanly unbelievable—that God is love for us—has happened in Jesus Christ. In the words of St. Paul to the Philippians: "His state was divine, yet he did not cling to his equality with God but emptied himself to assume the condition of a slave" (Phil 2:6-7). "Yes, but he was crucified through weakness, and still he lives now through the power of God" (2 Cor 13:4). Paul considers understanding and succumbing to God's incarnated love for man in Jesus Christ as the greatest and only ultimate knowledge that contains all other knowledge.

Origen beautifully describes the filling up of the sufferings of Christ, as Christ remaining on the cross as long as one sinner remains in hell.[23] Christ's love act on the cross is an everlasting act in *kairos,* that knows no end until man answers with a return of love. "And when I am lifted up from the earth, I shall draw all men to myself" (Jn 12:32). God makes known to individual human beings his infinite, personal love for us through the human love of Christ on the cross.

And yet when you ponder how you have met God in the beautiful gifts that God has sent into your life and how so many persons in history have been turned toward selfishness because of the society around them you begin to realize that the ever-loving Christ comes to you through his members in the Body of Christ. Would it be farfetched to believe that, what is utterly impossible for a person caught in the spiritual neuroticism of selfishness (and for him it is an eternal punishment of spiritual frustration of the God-given powers to love him and the whole world in him), could be possible through the working of God's merciful love?

A parable suggested by John A.T. Robinson might be helpful. He describes in the following way God's wearing down of man's resistance or, better, of man entering into true freedom of self-determination to love God in a total commitment of self.[24]

Two ways are eternally open to man. One road, crowded, full of people, leads to destruction. The other leads to true freedom in a conscious surrender of self to God. Somewhere along the first road, far or near from its beginning, man meets someone, a figure, stooping beneath the weight of the cross. "Lord, why are you doing this?" each of us some time or other asks. "For you, to prove that you are greatly loved by God." No person can indefinitely meet such great love, whether it is directly revealed through God's Word, Jesus Christ, or through beautiful, Christian persons who love those in hell with the very love of Christ. Man will not lose his choice to resist. He will want, like a feverish thirsting man on a desert, to stretch out to drink of this life-giving water. St. Paul says: "For God's foolishness is wiser than human wisdom, and God's weakness is stronger than human strength" (1 Cor 1:25). It is a fundamental paradox that only omnipotence can afford to become so weak, so humiliated in pursuing individual human beings so relentlessly.

God is God precisely because he is the perfection of all that we are in our limited possibilities. And man's greatest, most free, most human act is to love another unselfishly.

If you return love for love in this life or in the continued evolving life to come, it is not because you have first loved God. Rather, it is because, first and last, in our true, human, conscious adult life, God is ever-loving.

What is impossible to man is possible to God. From man's view, caught in the steel web of selfishness, there can be no way out, no exit from hell. Those in hell can only say with Albert Camus' lawyer in *The Fall*: "Fortunately I arrived! I am the end and the beginning; I announce the law. In short, I am judge-penitent."[25] But how God's great love for individual, intellectual beings, human and angelic, can operate and touch the frustrated beings in hell must only be cloaked in reverent mystery and hope. We need to hope that his mercy and love continue in the words of Jesus, the Image of God the Father, who asks continuously that they who did not know what they were doing would be forgiven (Lk 23:34).

Church historian Hans Lietzmann describes the hopeful eschatology of Origen who belived that evil, which was a nonexistent absurdity, eventually would be burned out of the hearts of those in hell and then God would be all in all:

> They will trace his guidance in their lives, feel his parental hand in their suffering and need, a hand which will not abandon even the last creatures of all in the deepest regions of hell. One after the other will be seized, accept conversion, mount slowly upwards joined by increasing numbers, and after inconceivable periods of time, the day will come when none will remain outside, and even when the prince of hell will return to God. Then the "return of the whole" will be completed, the purpose and meaning of the historical process fulfilled, death abolished, and Christ will place everything in himself and with himself at God's feet "in order that God might be all in all."[26]

Is Hell a Place?

To understand hell as Jesus taught it we must enter into the greatest mystery of all: the interacting between the humble, loving God towards all his children and man's unique free will to accept or reject God's love-gift of himself in Jesus Christ. To lose the mystery through objectification is to deny the basic doctrine Jesus taught and lived: God's love for us is infinite and endures forever. Thus the question of hell involves the most basic relationship between God and all individual human and angelic beings. It must be seen in all its terrifying aspects from our human view. This is what Jesus the preacher stressed and what the teaching church insists upon in maintaining the separation of the wicked from God, and from the eternal pain involved in such total frustration of our greatest human powers to love God and all other beings.

Hell truly exists. Such a relationship between God and man exists whenever man chooses over his life or at death, to orientate himself toward himself by refusing to love God in obedient service.

Have you ever visited a mental hospital and viewed human beings reduced in their neurotic sickness to prisoners caught inside their darkened and confused minds? Are they free to put aside their unreal world and begin to relate to their society around them in responsible love? Are they not "eternally" caught in a state of existence, unable to escape?

The mystery of God's ever-enduring love demands that the doctrine of hell also be viewed from God's relationship to us. By taking only the view of hell from man's side, theologians and preachers have forgotten the most important revelation of Jesus about his loving Father. Thus in our understanding of hell we pass over God's everlasting and actively involved love for us in order to portray God in his justice as a vengeful, vindictive despot. We have substituted a pagan god for the Father of Jesus!

Therefore, by asking the question: Is hell a place? you are forced to face the same problem. You can objectify from your human viewpoint and end up with a "place" created by God where individual souls are punished. Or you can retain the mystery of God's love and his relationship toward the wicked. Then such a place becomes man's inability to become "present" to God.

Robert Southwell, S.J., in a poem written in the 16th century, expresses how place in the spiritual realm of love is presence to the one loved: "Not where I breathe do I live, but where I love."

Love "localizes" you by allowing you through your spiritual powers, God's activating love operating through your intellect, will and emotions, to be present to as many persons as you unselfishly love. If hell describes the condition of "unloving," self-centered persons, then you can understand that God is present to them, but they are not present to God.

However, is there not a negative presence of such persons to each other in their terrifying spiritual neuroticism? Are they not present to a cosmic world that is a source of disharmony and of intense suffering to them? Karl Rahner brings out the cosmic suffering due to a person in hell who is present to a chaotic cosmos. "Fire is a metaphorical expression for something radically not of this world—but this does not mean that fire is to be given a merely psychological explanation. It does mean the cosmic, objective aspect of loss, which is outside the consciousness, a definitive contradiction of the abiding and perfected world, which will be a torment."[27]

Through death an individual not only continues to be present to the cosmos around him, but now in a spiritual manner of existing, he or she can be very present either in a loving, harmonious union as found among the saints, or in a disharmonious antagonism and enmity between the wicked and the rest of the cosmos. A peculiar relationship of enmity and self-centeredness would be experienced among the wicked. German theologian A. Winklhofer expresses well the "place" of the damned in regard to the surrounding, created world:

> If it is reasonable to understand by heaven
> the entire transfigured creation, and hell-fire

as the creation as inimical and alien to the
damned, we may well assume that hell is, by
God's mercy, a place set apart, "a prison"
(Rv 20:7), bounded not by walls but by in-
capability of the damned soul to apprehend
other parts of the cosmos. . . . The whole
vast creation may well be, for the damned it
torments, far smaller and more restricted
then it is for the blessed, whose unimpaired
faculties perceive and experience it in its
totality. Hell would then be, not a place
within the cosmos, "above" or "below," but a
particular constricted relation to the
cosmos. . . . "places" in the next world are a
metaphysical, not a spatial character. No
"way" leads to them, and neither is there
"distance" from them. We must be content to
say: hell is the damned person himself;
where he is, there is hell.[28]

From the view of the damned, there can be no way
out, no hope emanating from their free will determina-
tions to make new choices in love. Universalism is
another attempt to penetrate this great mystery of God's
love and man's free will to accept or reject his love by ob-
jectifying the mystery with an easy solution. This hardly
does justice to man's free will and the daily experience of
how we eventually become fixed in our value system.

Yet from God's view, in a mysterious manner that
escapes all human reasoning, He will always continue to
love each person made by him to share in his trinitarian
life. To believe that God's justice demands that he hate
the wicked and departs definitely from them with no
more concern, is to make a mockery of the God that
Jesus revealed to us. Let us take the example of a
neurotic, incapable of healing himself, yet of being
capable of experiencing some escape, some healing

through a loving, trustful psychiatrist or through a group of loving persons who ever so gradually lead the neurotic back to some normalcy.

Cannot God directly continue to reveal his immense love in the life to come as Jesus imaged that love by going among the broken human beings and healing them by his love? On whose authority can we ever dictate to God what he must do? Why must his love operate only until our death? If God were to cease loving in an active, involving way, would he be love by nature?

And furthermore, cannot God reveal his love for those in hell through his loving saints? St. Paul assures us that in the life to come all other things will pass away except love. "Love does not come to an end" (1 Cor 13:8). For those who have already entered into eternity in the love of God, heaven is where God is present. Yet their love burns within them to share the goodness of God with others. Again St. Paul assures us that the healthy members of the body come to the aid of any injured or needy members. "If one part is hurt, all parts are hurt with it" (1 Cor 12:26). In the Body of Christ, the healthy, saintly members come to the rescue of those who are injured. A sign of love is self-sacrificing service to the needy.

And who among all of God's creatures are more needy than those in hell? The saints desire to be all things to all men to win them to Christ, as St. Paul wanted to do. Why should love change in the lives of the saintly in heaven? Is it too farfetched to think that they love God by serving the broken ones, both those still on this earth and those in purgatory and hell? "For he must be King until he has put all his enemies under his feet and the last of the enemies to be destroyed is death, for everything is to be put under his feet" (1 Cor 15:26). This is the active, involving love of God working in his healthy members of the Body of Christ to wipe out any misery, so that the full Christ may enter into his glory.

Love Is Suffering

A favorite author of mine, Georges Bernanos, has made this sense of solidarity with sinners, to the point of voluntary substitution, the basis of true Christian holiness. He rather dramatically and even romantically pushes this kind of substitution in the experience of damnation in imitation of Christ on the cross. Perhaps his insights on this matter can help us to understand something of how God's infinite love may operate on those in hell in the life to come. Swiss theologian H. Urs von Balthasar has interpreted the theology of Bernanos in terms of ultimate love of Christ in the mystic conquering him to the point of "folly" in order to lead others to Christ. He writes:

> We have reached here the antipodes of that ascending contemplation, of the individualistic type, which has been more markedly impressed by the neo-Platonist stamp than by the spirit of the Gospel, which has wormed its way through the patristic and scholastic tradition, and which, even today, still constitutes the mystical schema highly favored in certain famous schools of theology. As far as Bernanos is concerned, true mysticism "does not resemble that which we read in books" *(La Joie, p. 230)*. It consists simply in this: that one allows himself to be thrown out of all shelter, not only out of worldly shelters, but even far away out of that supernatural security of the life of faith as guaranteed by the church herself. The true mystic is a man who lets himself be cast down into the abyss, where he is tossed about in all directions, in a kind of darkness where there is no distinction between up and down, for to be forsaken by the father is to be delivered into the hands of satan.[29]

In heaven the saints, even though they know they can never be damned because of their love for Christ, still know that their love must stretch itself to such heights of "folly" because of the great love unto folly that they have experienced from Jesus Christ. The more one is raised to this life in Christ, the more he enters into communion with all other human beings. There develops within him a genuine sense of being one with the whole world, created by God and loved by God as good. He is open and ready to give himself to this world and more specifically to the need in that world and in the world of hell. True love of God must make all of us into active lovers of all other human beings, including those suffering in hell. "As long as we love one another, God will live in us and his love will be complete in us" (1 Jn 4:12).

Those saints in heaven, who know that they are one in the Body of Christ and enjoy that same oneness with all those in the same fellowship in that Body, contemplate Jesus Christ as yet not formed in the lives of those who live in hell. They not only live in the hope that all persons will come to know Jesus Christ as the father's gift, but that they are the instruments whereby God actively brings his life-giving love to the needy. Jesus Christ is now achieving the victory over cosmic evils through all of his members on earth and those living in him in eternal life. He is precisely overcoming the forces of death, sin and chaos and is bringing about a gradual transfiguration of the entire creation of God.

Jesus in the Gospels and his church in its teaching, tell us that hell is real. It exists even in this life and continues in the life to come in anyone who freely rejects the love of God and lives only for him or herself. As Dante warns those who enter hell to put aside all hope of ever leaving such a place, so there can be no other choice on the part of the damned in that state of hellish existence. But it is totally beyond our imagination what God can do through his contemplatives, those who see the triune God dwelling within themselves, those who, in true Christian hope and love, strain to stretch out to those groaning in travail.

The holy ones of God, who have understood St. Paul when he wrote ". . . the only thing that counts is not what human beings want or try to do, but the mercy of God" (Rom 9:16), share in the pain of the Good Shepherd who searches for his lost sheep, not only on this earth, but in the farthest reaches of hell. For such, also for the early Christians, Jesus still descends into hell and there preaches the Good News.[30]

And such mystics can live in a paradox that insists on the definitiveness of man's free choices that can surely fashion him into the state of hell, and yet can insist also that the infinite mercy and love of God and his divinized saints can possibly touch the damned and, by love, heal them into well-adjusted citizens of the City of God.

Hell is a most important doctrine and may never really make sense to our puny human minds. But hell is conquered by us in this life as we yield to the reconciling power of Jesus Christ and the healthy members of his Body. And if it is to be conquered for those who have sentenced themselves to hell, it will not be by their own power, but by the power of the same Jesus Christ, the merciful Lamb of God, who takes away the sins of the world by being a pursuing love toward the broken and the miserable.

To this reconciliation he calls the members of his Body. They are to lay down their lives for such in hell. The question is not theirs to ask: "Will eventually all in hell accept God's love in Christ Jesus?" Theirs is only to show the love and mercy of Christ toward all who suffer and lie in darkness. Theirs is to be the light of Christ to the blind. Theirs is to release the love of God in Jesus Christ through their love toward the most despicable and forsaken beings. For they know that heaven is a state of happiness in God's love that is measured by death to self and a rising with Christ to love and serve the needy. Such love grows on sacrifice and self-giving. Greater union with Christ comes by service to the poor. "I tell you solemnly, in so far as you did this to one of the least of these brothers of mine, you did it to me" (Mt 25:40).

The states of heaven and hell cannot be separated since love breaks down all barriers of communication and builds reconciliation or loving union. The beautiful words of St. Paul form a fitting conclusion:

> And for anyone who is in Christ, there is a new creation; the old creation has gone, and now the new one is here. It is all God's work. It was God who reconciled us to himself through Christ and gave us the work of handing on this reconciliation. In other words, God in Christ was reconciling the world to himself, not holdings men's faults against them, and he has entrusted to us the news that they are reconciled. So we are ambassadors for Christ; it is as though God were appealing through us, and the appeal that we make in Christ's name is: be reconciled to God. For our sake God made the Sinless One into sin, so that in him we might become the goodness of God (2 Cor 5:17-21).

Chapter Eight
An Evolving Heaven

A group of scientists met in Mountain View, California at the Ames Research Center of the National Aeronautics and Space Administration to discuss the possibility of superior civilizations existing in other worlds than the one we know.[1] Dr. Dale A. Russell, a Canadian paleobiologist, pointed out that the present level of human intelligence might have been reached 60 million years ago, if the rapid evolution of nervous systems shown in the early development of life had continued.

A slowing down process, some 230 million years ago, took place, according to this report, but the cause is uncertain. This change coincided with the emigration of life forms from the sea to the land. Dr. Russell observed that if the subsequent, slower rate had prevailed throughout the history of life, it would have required 20 billion years to evolve human thinking capability. He concludes that the development of intelligence on other worlds may depend on those factors that made for the earlier, faster progress.

The beauty of God's creation is the intricacy of dependent life forms upon each other, through what Teilhard de Chardin called "the law of complexity." Matter is always moving toward spirit. The human person stands at the pinnacle of such an *elan vital,* possessing the highest form of consciousness thus far known on earth. He, above all other creatures, has been made according to God's very own image and likeness (Gn 1:26). He stands over and against his creator as a self-positing, free creature, as an *I,* capable of responding to God's invitation to become a sharer in his very own life (2 Pt 1:4).

The Psalmist cries out in humble amazement at God's goodness in sharing his creativity with man:

> Ah, what is man that you should spare a thought
>   for him,
> the son of man that you should care for him?
> Yet you have made him little less than a god,
> you have crowned him with glory and splendor,
> made him lord over the work of your hands,
> set all things under his feet,. . . (Ps 8:4-6).

Upward Progress

If the natural sciences can trace out the slow, evolutionary steps that led from lower forms of life, it is for psychology and religion to show the growth from the first stage of human consciousness to ever-increasing levels of human development and maturity. Such a growth in human consciousness and personal maturity must always be measured by a disintegration of a self-centered world and a reintegration of one's human life into the other-centered world.

Dr. Bernard J. Boelen defines human, personal maturity in terms of an individual's conscious movement outward toward a cosmic community. "It is impossible to define the mature personality unless one grasps the human person as a whole and understands his fundamental integration in the cosmic context of his meaningful relationships to the whole of Being."[2]

As God created the world, he meant all parts to be coordinated into a whole, into a dancing harmony. Man alone, created by God to know God's plan and to be a loving participant along with God's creative Word, was given stewardship over this wonderfully rich world. The world, from God's viewpoint, is a *one*. All creatures, through the creative inventiveness and synergism of man working with God, were meant to be interrelated in harmonious wholeness. Each part has its proper place within the whole universe. God creates, never to destroy, but to bring into a fuller richness and complexity in unity through love. Each creature depends on and gives support to all others in one great body, all of which has been created in and through God's Word.

How beautifully this is brought out in Psalm 104:

> Yahweh, what variety you have created,
> arranging everything so wisely!
> Earth is completely full of things you have made:
> among them the vast expanse of ocean,
> teeming with countless creatures,
> creatures large and small. . . .
> You give breath, fresh life begins,
> you keep renewing the world (Ps 104:24-25,30).

This wonderful, creating God is not only the powerful, transcendent creator who stands above and outside of all his creation, but he is the immanent force that lives inside of every creature. ". . .In him we live, and move, and exist. . ." (Acts 17:28). He fills the heavens and the underworld. It is impossible to escape from his creative, sustaining spirit (Ps 139:7).

God is so omnipresent because he is love. Love means being present to the one loved, not only in gifts given, words exchanged, gestures acted out of an interior state of oneness, but in actual union through total self-giving. The awesomeness of God is his infinite humility in desiring to give himself and to share his very own life with us.

Man—the Icon of God

Not only does God communicate himself through his innumerable gifts of creation, but he is a presence, a sustaining, directing force in his desire to be still more present to man. God's Word, through his creation, is continually being communicated over millions of years as man evolves into greater consciousness of his identity as a matured citizen of the cosmos.

Holy Scripture depicts God as a self-communicating community, freely deciding on a course of creative giving to human creatures, whom he specially endows with a potential to enter into knowledge of him and submit to him in loving surrender.

> God said, "Let us make man in our own image, in the likeness of ourselves, and let them be masters of the fish of the sea, the birds of heaven, the cattle, all the wild beasts and all the reptiles that crawl upon the earth" (Gn 1:26).

All other creatures are brought into being by God's imperative: "Let there be . . . ." Because of their fixed nature, God limits his communication with plants or animals. Only man is open-ended, God-oriented and capable of an evolving communication with him. In his first moment of existence, man is seen to be in communication with God. Scripture shows God speaking to man in the coolness of evening. Man's uniqueness, as the early Greek Fathers saw, was not in being the image of God, but in possessing an intellect and will. Man's uniqueness consists in being able to posit himself as an *I*, dependent on the Absolute *I* of God.[3]

Man has his full being in a conscious relationship to God in and through the only true image of God, Jesus Christ. We are made for a oneness with Christ and, in and through him, we are to respond to God's gift of himself just as he gives himself to his only-begotten Son through his Spirit. Our human self-realization through love is possible only because "God is love and anyone who lives in love lives in God, and God lives in him" (1 Jn 4:16). We are the overflow of God's fullness. In his utter selflessness because he is All, God's goodness creates us, not that he may receive a needed love in return from us, but in order that he may pour out of the infinite abundance of his being shared-life-in-love. This mystery, revealed to us by the eternal Word of the Father, assures us that we have been made by God out of love, in love and destined for love by participating in God's own life.

> And eternal life is this:
> to know you,
> the only true God,
> and Jesus Christ whom you have sent (Jn 17:3).

Christian revelation assures us that God's end in creating us is that we may share in his very own family life. Jesus teaches us in the New Testament that we can know and experience this Trinity by entering into a regeneration through the Holy Spirit, born from above (Jn 3:3), and obtain eternal life and happiness by returning this love to God by loving one another.

Jesus—the Way to Eternal Life

God reached a peak in becoming present and self-giving to us when he sent his only-begotten Son to become the way that leads us to eternal life.

> The word was made flesh,
> he lived among us,
> and we saw his glory,
> the glory that is his as the only Son of the Father,
> full of grace and truth (Jn 1:14).

The Divine Logos, Jesus Christ, God made flesh, is the supreme event of God's infinite condescension to communicate himself to mankind. Not only would he be the model, the image of his heavenly Father, according to which each individual person would be created, but he would actively effect, by the divine life of his Spirit dwelling in man through grace, that image into its fullness, into the very likeness of the Son of God himself. Jesus had promised such an indwelling relationship among him and his heavenly Father and the individual disciple who kept his commandments. That trinitarian life would make its home with the followers of Jesus (Jn 14:23).

God's glory has come down from the heavens in the person of Jesus Christ. "He is the radiant light of God's glory and the perfect copy of his nature, sustaining the universe by his powerful command; and now that he has destroyed the defilement of sin, he has gone to take his place in heaven at the right hand of divine Majesty. So he is now as far above the angels as the title which he has inherited is higher than their own name" (Heb 1:3-4).

He has descended among us in order that we might ascend with him to share in the glory of the sons and daughters of God (Eph 4:9-13). We have been given "the promise of an inheritance that can never be spoilt or soiled and never fade away, because it is being kept for you in the heavens" (1 Pt 1:4). St. Irenaeus and all the Greek Fathers that followed him expressed the work of Christ as the "recapitulation" or bringing to fulfillment of God's eternal plan to share his divine life with us. God became man in order that man might become god, and this by grace granted us through Jesus Christ and his Holy Spirit.

No one has captured the awesome plan of God Almighty as did St. Paul when he wrote the following words:

Before the world was made, he chose us, chose
    us in Christ,
to be holy and spotless, and to live through love
    in his presence,
determining that we should become his adopted
    sons, through Jesus
Christ for his own kind purposes,
to make us praise the glory of his grace,
his free gift to us in the Beloved,
in whom, through his blood, we gain our
    freedom, the forgiveness
of our sins. . . .
And it is in him that we were claimed as
    God's own,
chosen from the beginning,
under the predetermined plan of the one who
    guides all things
as he decides by his own will;
chosen to be
for his greater glory,
the people who would put their hopes in Christ
    before he came. . . .
and you too have been stamped with the seal of
    the Holy Spirit
of the Promise,
the pledge of our inheritance
which brings freedom for those whom God has
    taken for his own,
to make his glory praised (Eph 1:4-14).

The Heavenly Inheritance

By God's overwhelmingly gratuitous desire to share
his very own nature and trinitarian life with us, we are
called to enter into what Holy Scripture calls the kingdom
of God or, as expressed often in the Synoptic Gospels, to
enter into the kingdom of heaven. Heaven! That is the
name of our fatherland! It is the goal of all our human
yearnings, the fulfillment of all our desires.

Anthropologists have shown that every race and culture of human beings has professed a belief in an unending life of bliss and fulfillment of all human desires for those who live an upright life on earth. Our human imaginations have conjured up fantasies of heavens that suit the needs and desires of each person.

Belief in heaven is more than unending life after death. The full meaning and proper understanding of heaven can only be attained by means of divine revelation. Without God's revelation guiding us our musings about heaven are the stutterings and mumblings of children.

> For our knowledge is imperfect. . . but once
>   perfection comes,
> all imperfect things will disappear. When I was a
>   child,
> I used to talk like a child, and think like a
>   child, and
> argue like a child, but now I am a man, all
>   childish ways
> are put behind me. Now we are seeing a
>   dim reflection
> in a mirror; but then we shall be seeing face to
>   face.
> The knowledge that I have now is imperfect;
>   but then I shall know as
> fully as I am known (1 Cor 13:10-13).

Let us turn to Holy Scripture to see how the heavenly life is described. We wish to see the kind of heaven that Jesus Christ describes since our Christian faith believes that the heaven in which we are called to share is the same as that from which the Son of God descended. Only he who has been in heaven and has come down to this earth can adequately tell us what awaits us.

I tell you most solemnly,
we speak only about what we know
and witness only to what we have seen
and yet you people reject our evidence.
If you do not believe me
when I speak about things in this world,
how are you going to believe me
when I speak to you about heavenly things?
No one has gone up to heaven
except the one who came down from heaven,
the Son of Man who is in heaven (Jn 3:11-13).

Heaven in the Old Testament

Heaven in the Old Testament has two main meanings. It is used to describe all that physically is above the earth (in Hebrew, *samayim*). The Jews of the Old Testament accepted a threefold division of the universe: the heavens, the earth and the abyss of water under the earth—or the heavens, the earth and Sheol (cf.: Ps 115:16 ff.).[4] The heavens are like a huge inverted bowl whose rim rests on foundational pillars (2 Sm 22:8; Jb 26:11).

But heaven or the heavens in its religious meaning refers to the place where God dwells and from which we are to receive a share in his blessings. The earth has been given by God to men, but heaven belongs to him (Gn 1:28; Ps 8:6-10; Gn 11:5; 19:24; Dt 10:14; Is 64:1). Yet, even though God dwells up in the heavens, he still comes down and communes with human beings. He meets Moses or the Israelites at the tent of meeting (Ex 33:9). The earth contains some special places where God is found communicating himself to his people. This manner of speaking brings the transcendent God, living up in his heavens, down to earth through his words spoken to his people, especially through his prophets and his law and in the Holy of Holies.

The Israelites looked to heaven as the source of salvation and of all God's gifts (Dt 33:13). This heaven, as the Book of Genesis describes it, is the paradise or Garden of Eden where the first man and woman enjoyed the abundance of God's blessings before sin closed it to mankind. Still the chosen people waited expectantly for the day when God would open heaven again and pour down his blessings abundantly upon his people. "Oh, that you would tear the heavens open and come down. . ." (Is 64:1). The Jews gradually hoped that they somehow would also be lifted up to heaven to enjoy blissful communion with God (Ps 73:23-28). Such an "ascension" into heaven was accorded to Enoch (Gn 5:24) and Elijah (2 Kgs 2:11). The *Hesed* Covenant would be completed when man would also return to God in heaven.

Heaven in the New Testament

God's Word is pictured in the New Testament writings as literally descending from heaven to earth and then ascending back to heaven. Jesus Christ becomes the centering point where heaven and earth meet. He is the *Pontifex Maximus* who spans the distance between heaven and earth, uniting mankind again with God. In the Old Testament the Holy of Holies was the "place" where God came down to earth (Gn 28:12-17). Jesus is declared to be the new temple (Jn 2:19-22).

In John's Gospel, Jesus is depicted as coming down from heaven (Jn 3:13,31; 6:38 ff.). And all four Gospel narratives recount the heavens' opening at the time of Jesus' baptism along with the manifestation of the Father by the voice and of the Spirit by the dove (Mt 3:16-17; Mk 1:10-11; Lk 3:21-22; Jn 1:32-34).

What was hidden in mystery in God (Eph 3:9; Jn 1:18) was opened by the revelation of Jesus Christ.

Whoever saw him would see also the Father (Jn 14:9). God's glory was upon him and those who saw that glory were called to share it (Jn 1:14; Phil 3:20). By dying and showing the great love that the heavenly Father has for his children, Jesus was raised by that Father in glory. This is characterized in mythical language by the ascension of Christ to the right hand of the Father (Mt 26:64; Mk 14:62; Lk 22:69; Acts 7:55; Rom 8:34; Eph 1:20; Col 3:1; I Pt 3:22). Thus Jesus is the firstborn among many brethren (Rom 8:29) and he has gone ahead to prepare a heavenly mansion for each of his followers.

> There are many rooms in my Father's house;
> if there were not, I should have told you.
> I am going now to prepare a place for you,
> and after I have gone and prepared you a place,
> I shall return to take you with me;
> so that where I am
> you too may be.
> You know the way to the place where I am going
>   (Jn 14:2-4).

Christians, therefore, are in a period of expectant longing for the return of the Risen Jesus in his *Parousia* from heaven back again to earth to take his own with him to heaven (1 Thes 1:10; 4:16; 2 Thes 1:7; Phil 1:23; 2 Cor 5:6-8). Christ will lead them to the Father (Mt 25:34; 1 Cor 15:24). His chosen ones will live in the New Jerusalem (Rv 3:12; 21:2; 10-14). The risen, like Christ who is their prototype, are to be endowed with the qualities of the heavenly body: incorruptibility, glory, power and spirit (1 Cor 15:42-49).

Using many images drawn from Jewish apocalyptic literature of the intertestamental period, the authors of the New Testament books describe heaven as life eternal: the kingdom prepared from the foundation of the world; a marriage; the marriage of the Lamb and the bride; a great supper; the inheritance of the saints in light; an inheritance, incorruptible and undefiled, reserved in heaven; a better country; a prepared city; the heavenly Jerusalem; the holy Jerusalem coming down from God out of heaven; the tabernacle of God with men; a place of rest.[5]

The Glorious Presence of God

Even through such scriptural images our desire to comprehend heaven as the future goal of our earthly striving can never be satisfied. Preachers and writers often do a great disservice to Christ's teaching about heaven in yielding to the rather gross desire of their audience for a heaven of material delights. All too often, this image of heaven extends a selfishness, experienced on this earth, to an eternal possession of all sense pleasures and the absence of any pain. Jesus did not reveal all the details of heaven, but we can be sure that the kingdom of which Christ will be Lord and Master, will be a setting worthy of such a supreme king and, therefore, must always surpass infinitely our own expectations. Did not St. Paul tell us as much? "The hidden wisdom of God which we teach in our mysteries is the wisdom that God predestined to be for our glory before the ages began . . . the things that no eye has seen and no ear has heard, things beyond the mind of man, all that God has prepared for those who love him" (1 Cor 2:7-9).

Jesus walked while on this earth in the presence of his heavenly Father. He, who was one with God (Phil 2:6), grew daily in his awareness of heaven as the oneness in glory that he possessed in being the only-begotten Son of the eternal Father from all eternity, the oneness that was covering him and inundating every part of his consciousness. This oneness with his Father suffused his humanity as Jesus gently learned to exist in the truth of his Father's awesome transcendence in his life.

Jesus continually turned inwardly to find his Father at the center of his being (Jn 14:11) as the Father eternally begets him as his beloved Son. In the depths of his heart, his innermost consciousness, Jesus touched the Holy. The *Shekinah* of God's glory poured over him and allowed him in his humanity to share a oneness with the glory that was his with that of the Father from all eternity.

This hidden glory, that came from his vision of the heavenly Father loving him infinitely as his only-begotten Son, burst forth in the transfiguration of Christ before Peter, James and John.

The Greek Fathers call this the Taboric Light that had been always present within Jesus, but on this occasion (Mt 17:1-8; Mk 9:2-8; Lk 9:28-36; 2 Pt 1:16-18) it flashed out, blinding the disciples. They experienced something of heaven in the wisdom of Jesus glorified:

> . . . we had seen his majesty for ourselves. He was honored and glorified by God the Father, when the Sublime Glory itself spoke to him and said, "This is my Son, the Beloved; he enjoys my favor." We heard this ourselves, spoken from heaven, when we were with him on the holy mountain (2 Pt 1:16-18).

Jesus could tell us about heaven because he is "the Son of Man who is in heaven" (Jn 3:13). His transfiguration shows us that Jesus was always in heaven while on earth, because he was always one with the Father and his Holy Spirit. And he came to share his glorious resurrectional life with all human beings so that we, too, could "see" the triune God, a Semitic way of saying that we could become one, sharing the divine life of God. "Seeing" God is *knowing* him and this is eternal life (Jn 17:3). This knowledge goes beyond sense or intellectual knowledge derived by our own rational powers. It is experiential knowledge through faith, hope and love, poured as gifts into our hearts by the Spirit of the Risen Jesus, that transforms us into God's very own divine nature.

This faith vision is imperfect in this life, but in the life to come it constitutes the essential element of what heaven is truly all about. It is referred to as the beatific vision.

Beatific Vision

Most theologians before Vatican II, in teaching about the essence of our eternal happiness in heaven, described this in static terms of our "seeing" God's essence in the beatific vision. Such immobility was deemed the ultimate of God's perfection.

Therefore, the peak of our beatitude was seen to be an eternal gaze upon God's essence. Scholastic theologians spilled oceans of ink over the topics of essential and accidental beatitude and the primary and secondary objects of the beatific vision. They held that perfect happiness had to satisfy both our intellect in knowing God's essence intuitively and our will in loving God.

Christians today yawn before such seriousness as theologians battle among themselves to explain this beatific vision in terms of created actuation by Uncreated Act (de la Taille) or by quasi formal causality (Karl Rahner).

Our modern world explodes into such fresh and exciting richness that to consider heaven in any static and immobile terms has very little meaning today. Heaven as a place to which the saved go to gaze upon the essence of God through the beatific vision is being replaced by a more dynamic concept of a state of continued growth as God, angels and human beings lovingly interact to bring forth God's initial creation into ever-increasing beauty and harmony and unity.

Yet Holy Scripture and the traditional teaching of the church do present the goal of all human happiness to consist in a most intimate and immediate knowledge and love of the Trinity. How can we reconcile such knowledge and love of God with a dynamic growth process in building a richer, more beautiful universe?

To Share the Trinity

Christian revelation and our deepest human experiences tell us that we have all been made by God to live in a community of loving persons who call us into ever-increasing *being* by their self-sacrificing love. The Good News that Jesus preached and brought about by the pouring into our hearts of his Holy Spirit is that the kingdom of God is within us. This kingdom is a knowing and loving relationship, a sharing on our part through grace of the Trinity's very own nature along with the particular individual personhood of each person of the Trinity.

Jesus had promised such an indwelling, communitarian relationship among himself and his heavenly Father and the individual disciple who kept his commandments:

> If anyone loves me he will keep my word,
> and my Father will love him,
> and we shall come to him
> and make our home with him (Jn 14:23).

He had promised also to send his advocate, the Holy Spirit, who would come and abide also with his followers (Jn 14:26; 15:26; 16:7-8). The Holy Spirit, sent into our hearts by the Father through Jesus Christ, comes to seize us and take possession of us in order to give us to the Son. The Son leads us to the Father dwelling along with him in our hearts. The riches of the mystery of God are inexhaustible like an abyss. For who of us could ever plumb the depths of God's infinite love abiding within us?

Yet heaven is that state of knowingly and lovingly experiencing a share in that very trinitarian family. It is to let ourselves enter into the very movement of triadic life living within us. It is to swim in the powerful current of God's uncreated energies of love that completely surround us and permeate us as the ocean saturates a sponge.

By baptism we become incorporated into the very being of the Risen Lord, Jesus, who cannot be separated from the oneness that he shares in his very being with the Father and the Holy Spirit. The Spirit of Jesus reveals to us that we are really children of God and can call out *Abba* since we have become heirs of God and coheirs with Christ of heaven (Rm 8:15-16; Gal 4:6).

St. John, the beloved disciple of Jesus, is overwhelmed by God's loving condescension in wishing to share the sonship of Jesus with us by making us truly his very own children:

> Think of the love that the Father has lavished
> on us,
> by letting us be called God's children;
> and that is what we are. . . .
> My dear people, we are already the children
> of God
> but what we are to be in the future has not yet
> been revealed;
> all we know is, that when it is revealed
> we shall be like him
> because we shall see him as he really is (1 Jn
> 3:1-2).

We are called by God's predestination in his Son Jesus to become holy and blameless in his sight, to be full of love, to be his adopted children (Eph 1:4-5). God wishes us to become participants of his very own nature

(2 Pt 1:4). It is the Spirit who constantly reveals to us from within our true identity as children, loved infinitely by a perfect Father through Jesus Christ who has died for us. Yet when have we ever fully comprehended the awesomeness of our sharing in the very life and nature of the triune God?

St. Augustine, commenting on the words of Ps. 82: "You too are gods, sons of the Most High, all of you" (v.6), expresses well our ineffable human dignity as children of God:

> He who justifies is the very same who deifies, because in justifying us He makes us children of God. . . . Now, if we are children of God, by that very fact we are gods, doubtless not by a natural generation, but by a grace of adoption. One only, indeed, is the Son of God by nature, the one only God with the Father, our Lord and Savior Jesus Christ. . . . The others who become gods so become by his grace; they are not born of his substance so as to become what he is, but they attain to a divine sonship by the favor of his generosity, in order that they may be made co-heirs of Christ.[6]

This mystery of our entrance into the family of God to share in God's very own knowledge and love of each of the three Persons, uniquely different yet completely one, is the ultimate purpose in God's eternal plan of creation. We see this now very imperfectly, "darkly as in a mirror," writes St. Paul (1 Cor 13:12). We in this life can only experience this trinitarian life mediately, through images and concepts, through faith, hope and love.

But the essence of heaven will consist in seeing God as he is, "face to face" (1 Cor 13:12). You will understand in an intuitive, immediate grasp of knowledge and love the unity and diversity within the Trinity. You will then know how you can possess a human nature that still remains human and yet at the fullness of its human growth will be, at the same time, divine.

In the peace and joy of being one in the unity of the three Divine Persons, you will experience an ever-increasing, personal maturity through experiencing your unique personhood in the *I-ness* that is loved by the *Thou-ness* in each trinitarian Person in the total, unified *We* community. This uniquenesss will call out of you greater depths of love to serve God and others, the angels and saints, in order still more to enter into an ever-increasing oneness of all beings in God's Being.

A Motionless Movement

Far from being a static "vision" of gazing upon three immobile Persons of the Trinity, the beatific vision becomes a dynamic and exciting process of continued growth in love of God and love of neighbor. Caught up within the very dialectic of the Godhead, eternally moving from *Silence* to *Speech,* from perfect repose and motionlessness to sharing love in movement toward another, you, too, live in the blissful tension of peaceful repose and moving "towardness."

How exciting is the thought that heaven will be a state of continuous growth in loving "towardness" toward God and all of his creatures, especially in loving service toward other human beings. St. Gregory of Nyssa describes true perfection as "never to stop growing toward what is better and never to place any limit on perfection."[7] Grace or the life of God within human beings, both in this life and the life to come, presupposes growth in accepting a loving relationship with God. It is to accept the necessity of constantly moving toward God.

St. Gregory of Nyssa describes God's nature as goodness to be such that it entices the human soul to desire greater union and possession of the goodness for which it has been made. For this reason St. Gregory sees man's progress toward God as never-ending even in heaven. The first reason is that beauty, God himself, is infinite. The second is that the beautiful is of such a nature that the desire for it can never be really satisfied.[8]

> The soul, that looks up towards God and conceives that good desire for his eternal beauty, constantly experiences an ever-new yearning for that which lies ahead and her desire is never given its full satisfaction.[9]

This longing for greater union with God can never be a source of sadness when we human beings realize that our true satisfaction consists in constantly going on with our quest and never ceasing in our upward ascent. Each fulfillment of such a desire generates a further desire for the Transcendent.[10]

If God is love and is limitless in his goodness and love toward us, our desire must also be limitless. The very unrest, the stretching forth to higher perfection, greater union with the Trinity, such motion toward greater being, is the same as stability. Such spiritual movement is more than moving from one stage of perfection to another. It is more than a mere, static vision of God's beauty. God is eternally at rest; yet he exists always in an outgoing motion of love to share himself with the other.

After the contemplative has been purified in this life and in the life to come through the therapy of purgatory, to that degree he or she will stretch out ever more to God who attracts each soul continually to "keep rising ever higher and higher, stretching with its desire for heavenly things to those that are before (Phil 3:13), as the apostle tells us, and thus it will always continue to soar ever higher. . . . And thus the soul moves ceaselessly upwards, always reviving its tension for its onward flight by means of the progress it has already realized. Indeed, it is only spiritual activity that nourishes its force by exercise; it does not slacken its tension by action but rather increases it."[11]

Such spiritual growth, stretching in love toward greater union with the triune God, is what it means to be human. You become human, not only in the desiring, but by God's condescending giving of himself always in newer and more amazing ways to you who seek after him. "Happy those who hunger and thirst for what is right: they shall be satisfied" (Mt 5:6). That is why theologian Piet Schoonenberg can insist on a growth process in the life to come:

> A certain growth also remains possible in the final fulfillment. Otherwise we would perhaps cease to be human. Just as life constantly rediscovers itself from the past into the future, so we shall constantly rediscover our past and present in and from God in new and surprising ways.[12]

Can you, therefore, imagine that your purified, unselfish love for God will not enter into an ever-increasing, evolutionary growth in knowledge of God or loving surrender of self to God? Heaven is that condition wherein you exercise the human freedom to give yourself to God and to God in his world. Redemption could perhaps better be conceived of as, not a fixed state of beatific repose, but a growing process of discovering the love of God, both as manifested by his direct revelation of Self to us in his trinitarian relationships to us and as manifested in his participated beauty in creation, especially in his angels and blessed human beings.

Love of Others

If God is love, he must be always loving you in his activities. The Eastern Fathers from earliest times called the triune God—in his loving relationships of self-giving in his created order—uncreated energies of love. These are truly God and not something that reveals God to you.[13] St. Basil writes: "For God's energies descend down to us while his essence remains inaccessible."[14]

Unlike the Western approach to God's essence that in the beatific vision is fully and directly comprehended by the blessed, the Eastern Fathers retained always an "apophatic" approach that made God's essence accessible only to the triune Persons. We can all admit that, to fully comprehend God's nature, we would have to be God. Pope Benedict XII in his famous *Constitution* defined: that the blessed in heaven "do see the divine essence," and the Council of Florence defined the beatific vision as the blessed seeing "clearly the Triune God himself, just as he is." This would refer most likely to an immediacy of knowing and loving God on the part of the blessed, rather than a complete comprehension of his essence.[15]

Surely if the blessed comprehended God as he is, they all would enjoy him in the same, equal way. The Greek Fathers hold that there is no mediacy in the vision in heaven but that God is experienced in his self-giving. God can be known experientially and can be reached in union or deification. Thus is retained always an essential distinction between God and his creatures and yet there is the basis for union and a sharing in God's nature by participation in his uncreated energies which are God as he gives himself to his creatures.

With the divine energies always surrounding you, both in this earthly existence and in the transformed world of heaven, and always calling you to respond to

God's Word, you reach the highest development in your continued cooperation (synergy) with God's energetic presence. As you cooperate with God's grace as his divine, uncreated energies are manifested to you in the social context of your many-leveled relationships of body-soul-spirit in heaven, you will come to meet God and glorify him by your loving service toward other persons, both angels and human beings.

True contemplation and sanctity both in this life and in heaven must be measured exclusively by the degree of charity and humility possessed by the individual. The love of God experienced in deep contemplation "urges" you, to use St. Paul's strong term, to go out from yourself in humble service to all who need God's healing love, especially to loved ones and to those who are in most desperate need. This is the essence of the Christian vocation and the index of your share in the resurrectional life of the Risen Lord. Heaven can be no exception to the standard given us by Christ for life on earth, of measuring love for God by the love and service shown to your neighbor. You know whether God is in you by the love that you have for one another. True contemplation, and this is what the beatific vision ultimately is all about, is always begetting, becoming the other in greater unity of love that alone can be realized by humble service, interrelational involvement of self-giving toward the other.

Not only will you contemplate the self-giving, trinitarian persons within you but you will go out and discover that same trinitarian presence in other creatures. Your love will unite with the uncreated energies of God to cooperate with Jesus Christ and his Spirit in reconciling the whole universe to the Father in the fulfillment of all things in God. You not only wait for the completion of God's plan but the love of the indwelling Trinity prompts you, as a loving child of God, to cooperate in that work of transfiguring the whole universe.

What we are waiting for is what he promised:
the new heavens and new earth, the place
where righteousness will be at home (2 Pt
3:13).

Interacting Love

In heaven you will praise God and thank him constantly for his infinite goodness.

You will come to know how faithful he has been throughout your whole existence. In this earthly existence you can only accept his goodness and fidelity in faith, but in heaven you will have certitude of his great, immense love in action toward you and this will allow you to thank him with all the choirs of angels and saints as they, too, understand individually and corporately how good God is to all his creatures!

You will exchange knowledge of what God has done in your individual lives with all of the other blessed human persons and with the angels, with whom you now realize a oneness in the Body of Christ. In this intuitive knowledge of God's workings in all creation you can praise God eternally in and through his magnificent Word, Jesus Christ. He will not be a medium but he will be the direct expression of God's workings in love in your life. In him the Trinity is most perfectly manifested in all of the uncreated energies and in him you learn to love and serve God and neighbor. Such loving service constitutes the greatest expression of praise to the triune God, Father, Son and Holy Spirit.

You will praise God for his own being, his uncreated goodness as expressed in innumerable ways in the knowledge you shall have of the interacting love of the triune Persons. You will praise God for his uncreated energies as they go forth continually in an ongoing creation of the universe that, "from glory to glory," reveals ever more of God's perfections. "The heavens declare the glory of God" (Ps 19:1).

> Celebrating your acts of power
> one age shall praise your doings to another.
> Oh, the splendor of your glory, your renown!
> I tell myself the story of your marvellous deeds.
> Men will proclaim your fearful power
> and I shall assert your greatness;
> they will celebrate your generous kindness
> and joyfully acclaim your righteousness (Ps 145:4-7).

You will praise the Trinity, especially for God's self-giving in the gifts of his angels and saints, for all of his intelligent creatures. Constant praise will be on your lips as you glorify God in the humanity of Jesus Christ, the meeting of the divine and the human. Mary, the mother of God, will be seen in all of God's wonderful workings of grace and purity, in her total self-giving because God poured the fullness of grace, his trinitarian energies of love, into her throughout her whole lifetime of cooperating with the Word of God. The angels will be seen in their loyalty and fidelity in being the instruments of God's governing and directing presence throughout the entire cosmos.

Gift of Loved Ones

You will praise God especially for the gifts of your parents, relatives and dear friends who will eternally share with you, not only past generous love, but continuously new ways of loving you. Husbands and wives will meet and grow in greater love for each other as they praise God in that very love. Mothers will be united again with their children and their love will grow as they discover God at the heart of old and new ways of self-giving. Lovers will meet and know each other in God's eternal love. Then truly you shall understand intuitively the words of St. John as you know and experience the love of God in others:

> . . . as long as we love one another
> God will live in us
> and his love will be complete in us. . . .
> God is love
> and anyone who lives in love lives in God,
> and God lives in him (1 Jn 4:12, 16).

In heaven fear will be replaced by love. Gone will be the aggressive attacks on others, replaced by a Christlike gentleness as you open up to receive God's diaphanous presence shining toward you through the prisms of each human and angelic spirit encountered. The God in you embraces the God in the neighbor and you respond with excitement of always new discoveries of God's beauty in your oneness in Christ. No longer is the other a stranger. He or she becomes your brother and sister, a part of God's body! They are a part of you. You discover yourself in such a love movement.

No longer will there be two commandments: to love God and then to love your neighbor. If you truly are loving God and experiencing his love for you, you will be loving God in all persons and experiencing his love as you accept their love. And each love relationship will be unique and God-revealing. Such love experienced will call out a new impulse to give yourself lovingly in service to others. You will be able to share all of your past experiences, education, travel, that beautiful sunset up in the mountains, skiing down the slopes of the Rockies, the presence of God in deep, personal prayer. You will develop even further your talents and abilities in loving service. Think of the development in your own life as you encounter musicians of the caliber of Beethoven, artists and sculptors like Michelangelo, the beautiful and famous saints Peter and Paul, John and James, the martyrs Ignatius of Antioch and Stephen and all of the unknown saints who loved God in hidden fidelity! Politicians, scientists, writers, explorers, musicians, dancers, artists, persons of all talents will develop their gifts even more than they did in this earthly existence and be able to share them with you and you with them. Everyone will be content with his or her other charisms. In heaven there will be no jealousy or competition but only loving service.

The Place of Heaven

We have seen descriptions of heaven in the Old and New Testaments that employ spatial terms as though heaven were a place from which Christ comes and to which he and we some day will go. We realize such descriptions are merely symbolic, similar to the imagery in the Book of Revelations. Heaven is depicted as the New Jerusalem, the city of God, adorned with precious stones of diamond, crystal, agate, pearls and so forth (Rv 21:15-21). But in heaven there can be no space since there can be no extended matter. Yet there must be some localizing of individual consciousnesses and personalities. The total being of a human being and an angel, of the humanity of Christ and the glorified humanity of Mary, must be "localized" in some new experience of being in place, in being toward others. We will discuss the resurrected, glorious body in the next chapter. But in the doctrine of the risen body of Christ and the glorious, assumed body of Mary, the church teaches us that the whole person is present in heaven. The glorified body of each person is present to other "bodied" beings, now spiritualized, by the degree of love that each person has toward the other.

Karl Rahner writes: "It is *a priori* senseless to ask where heaven is if by this 'where' we are to understand a location in *our* physical spatial world."[16] We cannot imagine what a spiritual body will mean in being toward other spiritualized beings. We can believe that the material world of plant and animal life and inanimate life will also share in a spiritualizing process of transformation through the activities of God, angels and human beings, but it is impossible to imagine in this life how spiritualized beings will be limited and contained within the boundaries of their unique being. This is a mystery that will have to await us in heaven when our corruptible bodies will have put on incorruptible ones (1 Cor 15:53). It will be a part of our happiness, but it will flow out of the greater happiness of being one in Christ with the Father and his Spirit.

Love Does Not End

Heaven is the ultimate experience of the life of faith that began on this earth with baptism. Heaven is of one piece with the life you live on this earth. The same relationships of love that called you into being will not only be present but will continue to call you into new levels of being for all eternity. Heaven is the beginning of true life, the fruition after the seed has dropped into the ground and died. It is a process of "further up" and "further in," into the heart of God who is at the heart of all things. It is the dance unending in which you grow in the rhythm of God.

Heaven is the continued process of knowing and loving God as our source. This is another word for *mysticism* in its fullest meaning. It is resting in God as the ultimate. It is stretching forth in concern and in loving service to bring light to darkness. Existentialist philospher Martin Heidegger expresses the essence of heaven in a short essay entitled "The Pathway":

> Growing means this: to open oneself up to the breadth of heaven and at the same time to sink roots into the darkness of earth. Whatever is genuine thrives only if man does

justice to both—ready for the appeal of highest heaven and cared for in the protection of sustaining earth.[17]

For such a truly realized human being, the true contemplative you are called to be, you and the whole world form a unity, "as beautiful as a bride all dressed for her husband" (Rv 21:2). You have your feet planted on this earth and yet you stand before the throne of God. You humbly utter the silent prayer in loving gratitude: "There is only Christ: he is everything and he is in everything" (Col 3:11). You stand in heaven before the throne of God and hear the Word of God speak to you of heaven as already begun on this earth:

You see this city? Here God lives among men. He will make his home among them; they shall be his people, and he will be their God; his name is God-with-them. He will wipe away all tears from their eyes; there will be no more death and no more mourning or sadness. The world of the past has gone. Then the One sitting on the throne spoke: "Now I am making the whole of creation new," he said, "Write this: that what I am saying is sure and will come true." And then he said, "It is already done. I am the Alpha and the Omega, the Beginning and the End. I will give water from the well of life free to anybody who is thirsty; it is the rightful inheritance of the one who proves victorious; and I will be his God and he a son to me" (Rv 21:3-7).

Chapter Nine
I Await the Resurrection of the Dead

I have often wondered why Christian liturgical art has never made much of the butterfly. It may be only my personal whim, yet it seems to me that that beautiful, free creature, as it so busily flies from flower to flower, doing good wherever it goes, should have served liturgical artists as a symbol of Christian resurrection.

Like Christians who reach the glorious, risen state of living in Christ, the butterfly was not always such a beautiful creature. It evolved from a lowly caterpillar, a creature not very beautiful to behold, certainly not very free in its slow, crawling efforts to get somewhere. But the butterfly was being formed when the caterpillar spun its prison-like cocoon and entered into the chrysalis stage.

In womb-tomb confinement, slowly, a new and more beautiful creature is being fashioned. The cocoon is split along its side and the butterfly emerges, wings wet and tightly packed. It stretches out its wings. It flies off—a new creation; one that hardly resembles the caterpillar at all. Yet all that beauty was locked in hidden potential within the ugly little caterpillar.

From the moment of our conception in our mother's womb, we, too, are launched on a course of evolution. There is a bodily development that is very dependent for its full growth on outside factors, such as the genes of our parents orientating us toward this or that type of body, on food and drink and care. But there is in all of us a psychic and spiritual development that requires very much our loving cooperation if we are to reach new levels of human perfection.

Evolution Toward Eternal Life

In baptism we Christians became like a seed, implanted in the church. There we were to grow to full maturity as children of God, as living members of the Body of Christ. A transfiguring process was to take place over the spring, summer and autumn years of our Christian lives, as we in faith, hope and love yielded to the transforming and divinizing power of God's Spirit.

We profess in the Nicene Creed that we look forward to the resurrection of those who have died. The Apostles' Creed professes belief "in the resurrection of the body." When resurrection is dealt with in the New Testament as the final stage of our human development, it usually refers to the resurrection of the dead (e.g. 1 Cor 15:12 ff.; 21-42; Acts 24:21; Heb 6:2) and not merely the resurrection of the body.[1]

The Christian concept of resurrection embraces what happened to Jesus Christ after his death on the cross and what happens to every one of us after our earthly death. Its belief is rooted in the Old Testament understanding of man as a total oneness, an embodied being. As we have seen, such a concept of biblical man as a total entity, a gift from God of a person of both body and spirit relationships (Gn 2:7), is foreign to the Platonic idea of man as a soul in a body. Thus the Hebrew understanding of man in death is not that of a body that dies and an immortal soul that separates from the dead body. Rather, it lays the foundation for our Christian belief that the whole human person undergoes death and the whole being will rise to a new creation in the process called resurrection.

In order to come to a true Christian understanding of resurrection, one that can be purified from the Platonic or Jewish apocalyptic imagery, we must turn to the resurrection of Jesus Christ.

The Kingdom of God

If you are to see the resurrection, both of Jesus and of yourself, as the peak of human development, you must begin with the preaching and person of Jesus when he was on this earth. St. John's Gospel presents Jesus as the preexistent Logos of God who "was made flesh" (Jn 1:14) as the Father's gift of love for us so that, if we believe in him, we should never perish but would enjoy eternal life (Jn 3:16;10:10; 17:3).

In the Synoptic Gospels Jesus preaches the essential elements in his redemptive work among mankind. He came to establish the kingdom of heaven through his sufferings and death and also through his resurrection (Mt 16:21; 17:22-23; 20:17-19; Lk 24:46-47; Mk 16:14-15). St. Luke carries these themes into the first chapter of Acts where Jesus is described as manifesting himself and telling his followers about the kingdom of God and his promise of the Holy Spirit who would bring about the kingdom in their lives (Acts 1:3-5). These three elements, the kingdom of God, the death of Jesus and the resurrection of Jesus, are intimately connected with one another. The kingdom of God in its definitive stage of development would reach its fullness in and through the death and resurrection of Jesus.

The kingdom of God that Jesus announced was like a small seed that fell upon the earth (Mk 4:3-20). It grew imperceptibly, slowly, day and night. God's loving, inner energy, transforming human beings into sharers of his very own nature (2 Pt 1:4), grows mysteriously within you as you cooperate in your desire to surrender to God's presence in your life. But the power of growth, the fruits, come from God's loving Spirit.

To enter into a living experience of God as our loving Father, Jesus taught the necessity of a conversion, a *metanoia*. Jesus preached a turning away from one's self-absorption and a turning totally to God. Such a repentance is a gift that God gives to those who earnestly go out of self to seek God. It does not consist in certain rituals or things done. It is primarily a turning within so as to effect an inner revolution.

You must be "reborn" of the Spirit that Jesus would send you.

> I tell you most solemnly,
> unless a man is born from above,
> he cannot see the kingdom of God.
> . . . unless a man is born through water and the Spirit,
> he cannot enter the kingdom of God . . .(Jn 3:3,5).

This conversion is a "losing" of one's life, a movement away from the false *ego*, a surrendering completely to God as the inner, directing force in one's life. The seed has to die of its own self-containment and then it will bring forth new life, a rich harvest (Jn 12:24-25). It is a movement, a slow process whereby God becomes the revolving axis in your life. It is an enlightenment that is given by God to those who open up as earth to receive God's word. It not only shows you the meaninglessness of worldly, self-centered values but it also reveals the joy of surrendering to God's holy will in all your decisions. The enlightenment continues to create in you new depths of awareness of your own spiritual impoverishment that lead to a yearning to live by God's desires.

Son of Man

Jesus chose the title "Son of Man" from chapter seven of the Book of Daniel to associate himself with the glorious, final establishing of the kingdom of God.

> And I saw, coming on the clouds of heaven,
> one like a son of man.
> He came to the one of great age
> and was led into his presence.
> On him was conferred sovereignty,
> glory and kingship,
> and men of all peoples, nations and languages
>   became his servants.
> His sovereignty is an eternal sovereignty
> which shall never pass away,
> nor will his empire ever be destroyed (Dn
>   7:13-14).

Jesus, like John the Baptist, preached repentance in order to be saved. But Jesus preached the Good News that the kingdom of God was close at hand (Mk 1:15). The good news was not only that God was a loving Father of infinite mercy, forgiving each person his sins, bringing healing love to the lonely and desolate, hope to the hopeless, but that the in-breaking of God's energies of love into human lives was at that moment being brought about by this man, Jesus of Nazareth. "For, you must know, the kingdom of God is among you" (Lk 17:21).

Jesus, the Son of Man, was identifying himself with the kingdom of God (Mk 8:38-9:1; Mt 16:28; Lk 18:29). He was the Way, the Truth and the Life (Jn 14:6). No one could come to the Father except through him. Seeing him was the same as seeing the Father (Jn 14:9). The signs of the coming of the kingdom of God as prophesied by the prophets of old were being fulfilled by Jesus as he healed the sick, drove out devils, forgave sins. "But if it is through the finger of God that I cast out devils, then know that the kingdom of God has overtaken you" (Lk 11:20).

His disciples were to cure the sick and say, "The kingdom of God is very near to you" (Lk 10:9). The scribes and Pharisees, like Paul himself before his conversion, found something very dangerous about this man Jesus and his talk of the kingdom. If the kingdom of God is already here, unseen by signs, growing in a mysterious way that is outside of any legal control, of what purpose is their religion of ritualism and externalism? Little by little they began to see that this man Jesus was claiming, not that he was the king of the kingdom, but that he was the presence of God's dynamic power and force, bringing about new, life-giving relationships directly with God.

Suffering Servant

The fullness of the kingdom of God and the coming in glory of the Son of Man were interrelated. Jesus' miracles and healings were the signs that God's kingdom was already being fashioned. But before Jesus could come into his glory and the kingdom of God could reach its completion, something terrifying had to happen. It was not so great a price to be paid to purchase this kingdom. It was an evolution in the dynamics of the growth of the God-life in man through death to selfishness.

Jesus predicted three times in the Synoptic Gospels that before he could enter into his glory and be risen, he had to suffer and die an ignominious death. The glorious return of the Son of Man of Daniel had to evolve out of the Suffering Servant (*Ebed Yahweh*) of Isaiah (Is 42:1-9; 49:1-11; 50:4-11; 52:13; 53:12).[2]

For how long have theologians presented us with this image of Jesus: He suffered and died and then, after his soul separated from his body, on the third day his soul reentered his body and he left the tomb. The resurrection is conceived in Platonic terms of a resuscitation of Jesus' body and soul. The empty tomb is the proof for all sincere persons that Jesus is truly divine, for only God can raise the dead, in this case, himself, from the dead. We Christians can easily enough "handle" such a resurrection. It puts no burden upon us to accept such a God-man. We do not have to have much faith to conceive of a similar resurrection when our souls will return to our bodies on general resurrection day.

But this is not the resurrection and exaltation of Jesus as found in the witness of the early Christians, as recorded in the New Testament. When you separate Christ's resurrection from his sufferings and death and place your own resurrection in the far distant future (even to the end of the world!) without any intrinsic, dependent relationship with your present existence, then you have destroyed true Christian eschatology. John Macquarrie rightly observes: "Eschatology has been existentially neutralized when the end gets removed to the distant future."[3]

Jesus said: ". . . for as the lightning flashing from one part of heaven lights up the other, so will be the Son of Man when his day comes. But first he must suffer grievously and be rejected by this generation" (Lk 17:24-25). His sufferings and death were intimately linked with his exaltation (Mk 10:36-40). We often see that he links his death and resurrection with the fulfillment of the kingdom of God (Mk 8:31-32; 9:9-12; 10:32-34). This is certainly St. Luke's understanding of the sufferings and death and resurrection of Christ when he wrote:

> You foolish men! So slow to believe the full message of the prophets! Was it not ordained that the Christ should suffer and so enter into his glory? Then starting with Moses and going through all the prophets, he explained to them the passages throughout the scriptures that were about himself (Lk 24:25-27).

In the songs of Deutero-Isaiah, you have the prophetic vision of the Suffering Servant of Yahweh. When Jesus was baptized by John in the Jordan, he humbled himself to be reckoned among sinners. He heard his Father's voice from heaven: "This is my Son, the Beloved; my favor rests on him" (Mt 3:17). This is the introduction to the first song of the Servant of Yahweh: "Here is my servant whom I uphold, my chosen one in whom my soul delights" (Is 42:1). Jesus had come to serve and not to be served.

It was clear in the consciousness of Jesus, made more detailed as he met the unfolding will of his Father each moment of his earthly life, that his service to the Father was a service on behalf of God's people. That service, in God's eternal plan, was to be pushed to such self-forgetting that Jesus would be brought to a free gift of himself on behalf of the human race. There developed in Jesus an urgent sense that eventually his service to mankind would be made real when he would lay down his life for all human beings through the entire universe.

The *kerygma* or preaching of the early church, as found in the Gospels and Pauline writings, clearly attests to the necessity for Jesus to serve unto humiliating death so that he might enter into glory. On Pentecost St. Peter preached: "For this reason the whole House of Israel can be certain that God has made this Jesus whom you crucified both Lord and Christ" (Acts 2:36).

In Mark's Gospel Jesus openly preaches: ". . . the Son of Man was destined to suffer grievously, to be rejected by the elders and the chief priests and scribes, and to be put to death, and after three days to rise again . . ." (Mk 8:31). Peter, like so many of us, wanted a glorious, risen Jesus but without suffering because he (and we also) did not like to suffer. Evidently such service unto death was a part of God's plan. And if anyone would wish to be a part of Jesus, he must go against his selfishness, "lose his life," for in losing one's life for the Gospel he will "save it" (Mk 8:35).

On another occasion Jesus repeated the prediction of his suffering and death. His disciples had been arguing among themselves about who was the greatest. "If anyone wants to be first, he must make himself last of all and servant of all" (Mk 9:35). To follow Jesus, who is a servant like a child, you must also be like a child, little in your self-esteem, great in your loving service toward others.

A third prediction of his humiliating death is followed by another exhortation to suffer out of humble service to one another. James and John, the sons of Zebedee, wanted places of glory next to Jesus. His answer reveals not only his own mission as Suffering Servant but that of all called to discipleship:

> . . . anyone who wants to become great among you must be your servant, and anyone who wants to be first among you must be a slave to all. For the Son of Man himself did not come to be served but to serve, and to give his life as a ransom for many (Mk 10:43-45).

John the Evangelist, who makes much of the parallelism between Jesus and the Passover Lamb (Jn 1:29), surely must have had in mind the lamblike characteristics that Deutero-Isaiah attributed to Yahweh's servant.

> Harshly dealt with, he bore it humbly, he never opened his mouth, like a lamb that is led to the slaughter-house, like a sheep that is dumb before its shearers never opening its mouth (Is 53:7).

Kenotic Love

The outstanding scriptural text that links Jesus' death on the cross with a humble obedience to the Father is the famous early Christian hymn St. Paul presents in Phil 2:6-11. Here Paul implies strongly a free choice on the part of Jesus, not only to be the servant, but also freely to go all the way in obedience to the Father's decree in giving himself over to death. From such an emptying *(kenosis),* he would be exalted in glory by the Father.

His state was divine,
yet he did not cling
to his equality with God
but emptied himself
to assume the condition of a slave,
and became as men are;
and being as all men are,
he was humbler yet, even to accepting death,
death on a cross.
But God raised him high
and gave him the name
which is above all other names
so that all beings
in the heavens, in earth and in the underworld,
should bend the knee at the name of Jesus
and that every tongue should acclaim
Jesus Christ as Lord,
to the glory of God the Father (Phil 2:6-11).

This statement of the first Christian communities professes that Jesus was equal with God, but out of loving service toward us, he surrendered the glory, the *Shekinah,* of God's powerful presence in him. He did this in order that he could be in all things like us. "God dealt with sin by sending his own Son in a body as physical as any sinful body, and in that body God condemned sin"

(Rom 8:3-4). He was tempted as we are (Heb 4:15). His love for us was so great that there was nothing to distinguish him from ordinary people. He lived in an obscure village of Nazareth for 30 years, working as a carpenter. He knew hunger, thirst and fatigue. He grew in human knowledge, how to make things, cope with life's problems; above all, how to experience his Father's love in the love he gave to and received from the women and men who came into his life as his friends.

And, yet, as he grew in consciousness of who he was and what the Father was asking of him, he continually rejected his own will in complete submission and obedience to his Father's will. He disregarded the shamefulness of the cross (Heb 12:2), enduring it for love of us and for this reason the Father exalted him, giving him the name of Lord of the universe, allowing him to be called by the name no man could utter, *vere Deus*, Yahweh.

From the Cross to Glory

Can we not say, therefore, that Jesus, becoming the Suffering Servant of Yahweh, freely wants to suffer only because he wanted his human mind to be the perfect reflection of the divine mind? His human consciousness was to become one with the consciousness of the Father. Jesus in his service to the world, entering into the very depths of sin and death and utter emptiness of self, was choosing humanly to be like God. It was the most perfect plan of imaging the eternal love of the Father for you and me. We have no other way of knowing the Father but through the Son. Here you have the perfect expression in human language of the very being of God.

If God appears as Love in the manger at Bethlehem, how much more does he appear as Love in the stark poverty, humiliation and contempt of the cross? This act of freely choosing to be one with sinful humanity in order to receive the penalty for sins in the most dramatic emptying (*kenosis*) of the death on the cross, is the most graphic act of loving service toward all human beings.

We see the relationship of his sufferings on our behalf and his glorification, along with our own participated glorification, if we obey him as noted in the following words:

> Although he was Son, he learnt to obey through suffering; but having been made perfect, he became for all who obey him the source of eternal salvation and was acclaimed by God with the title of high priest of the order of Melchizedek (Heb 5:8-10).

When Jesus hung on the cross, as reported by Mark's Gospel (undoubtedly one of the earliest accounts given in the Christian community), he screamed out: "My God, my God, why have you deserted me?" (Mk 15:34). The emptying of the Suffering Servant of Yahweh had reached its peak. God was being manifested for each of us as Love, perfect in his self-surrender. "A man can have no greater love than to lay down his life for his friends" (Jn 15:13). And we might add, "Nor can God!" God reaches the peak of speaking his word. He can be no more present as Love than in his Image, Jesus Christ, poured out on the cross, even to the last drop of blood, made sin, rejected and outcast.

Hope for Meaningfulness

Death for all of us is the greatest threat to a meaningful existence. If Jesus were tempted in all things as we are and yet was without sin (Heb 4:15), he must have met his greatest temptation on the cross. In the face of the imminent death that slowly choked life from every cell in his body, Jesus, as all of us, must have wondered about the meaningfulness of his life, the years of monotonous living at Nazareth, the preaching unto fatigue only to be clawed by the broken ones of the earth who wanted his healing touch and then, his agony and crucifixion. What would be the effect on the lives of his disciples, his friends, on the Jews, the Greeks, the barbarians, on every last human being, of his suffering to serve them, to prove his personal love for each of them?

He learned obedience to his Father and love was created in his heart for all of us as he hoped that his sufferings and death would bring life to every man, woman and child created by his Father according to him, the Father's own image (Col 1:15). Jesus freely gave himself in life and in death to serve others. On the cross, when hope seemed all but extinguished that his sacrifice would be meaningful to the human race, the Father "raised him high" (Phil 2:9). The resurrection of Jesus must not be diluted of its power and true glory by relegating it to a return of his soul to his body. Nor is the resurrection simply the historical person, Jesus, continuing as if he had not died.

The whole Jesus died, not merely his body. The whole Jesus gave himself for love of each of us. And the Father raised him to new life and we also can now share in his new life.

> Blessed be God the Father of our Lord Jesus Christ, who in his great mercy has given us a new birth as his sons, by raising Jesus Christ from the dead, so that we have a sure hope and the promise of an inheritance that can never be spoilt or soiled and never fade away, because it is being kept for you in the heavens (1 Pt 1:3-4).

God has brought Jesus back from the dead "to become the great Shepherd of the sheep by the blood that sealed an eternal covenant . . ." (Heb 13:20). Joy is everywhere evident in the New Testament because Jesus has gone forward into a completely new existence which he now makes possible to share with his followers. "I was dead and now I am to live forever and ever, and I hold the keys of death and of the underworld" (Rv 1:18).

St. Paul clearly articulates the role of Christ's resurrection in our redemption: ". . . Jesus who was put to death for our sins and raised to life to justify us" (Rom 4:25). Jesus "died and was raised to life" (2 Cor 5:15) for you that you might have eternal life. In St. Paul's classical text, showing how Christ's resurrection is part of your salvation from sins, he writes, ". . . and if Christ has not been raised, you are still in your sins" (1 Cor 15:17).[4]

Pauline scholar Ernst Kasemann summarizes the glory of Jesus in his resurrection as his ability to lead his disciples on earth to share in his death and resurrection process:

> For Paul the glory of Jesus consists in the fact that he makes his disciples on earth willing and capable to bear the cross after him, and the glory of the church and of Christian life consists in the fact that they have the honor of glorifying the crucified Christ as the wisdom and power of God, to seek salvation in him alone, and to let their lives become a service to God under the sign of Golgotha. The theology of the resurrection is at this point a chapter in the theology of the cross, not its supersession.[5]

A New Creation

The act of Jesus dying and rising to a new, glorious existence could not have been comprehended by any human being since it was a happening outside of man's experience of history (*chronos* in Greek). Noted theologian Jurgen Moltmann shows how Jesus is inserted into human history through the resurrection that shatters all historical categories.[6] Only those who were open to the presence of Jesus in faith were able to truly "see" him as risen, to experience his glory and to know that they were sharing in that same resurrectional glory. Jesus could not have been seen in the same way by those who did not believe in him. He became present to his disciples in a new and more involving way. Jesus is now Lord of the universe and God of all. In the witness of doubting St. Thomas, we move also from historical knowledge to eschatological faith as he falls down to adore Jesus glorified: "My Lord and My God!" (Jn 20:28).

The early Christian community was saying in effect through the words put on the lips of the risen Savior: "Do not cling to me as you formerly knew and loved me. . . . Go and find the brothers and there you will also discover me in the only way I wish to be present to you" (Jn 20:17). St. Luke has Jesus physically present to the two disciples on the road to Emmaus, yet they did not recognize him until they broke the bread in faith. Luke's message is that the Word of God is present and recognized as such, not by seeing him, but by hearing the Christian community that gathers together through Jesus' Spirit and that speaks that Word in continuity with God's revelation in Tradition, both of the Old and New Covenant. There can be no contact with the glorious, risen Jesus except in his Body, the church, which in space and time now makes him present to us.[7] Jesus is also present in the church's action as the church "re-presents" Jesus in the Eucharist for the believers (1 Cor 11:23-29).

Christ's Victory

Jesus' victory over sin and death can be seen only in his members as they accept the good news of his victory and as they allow him, through his Holy Spirit, to enter into his glorious, eternal life by the forgiveness of their sins and sharing in God's divine life. Jesus in his risen humanity is the first benefit of the new creation, the new Adam, and he holds out to all of us a rebirth unto new life through his Holy Spirit.

> . . . it was for no reason except his own compassion that he saved us, by means of the cleansing water of rebirth and by renewing us with the Holy Spirit which he has so generously poured over us through Jesus Christ our savior. . . to become heirs looking forward to inheriting eternal life (Ti 3:5-7).

Death came through one man; but through the victory of Jesus in his resurrection from the dead you have been assured that you will rise in glory with him (1 Cor 15:21-23). You shall never die again because through Christ our corruptible nature has put on incorruptibility, your mortal nature now has immortality. "Death is swallowed up in victory. Death, where is your victory? Death, where is your sting?. . . So let us thank God for giving us the victory through our Lord Jesus Christ" (1 Cor 15:55-57).

The victory that the resurrection of Jesus brings is the knowledge of the Father and Jesus his son through the Holy Spirit, a knowledge that brings eternal life and a share even now in the resurrection of Jesus (Jn 17:3). This knowledge is received in prayer and is experienced every time you live in self-sacrificing love for another person, knowing the infinite love of God in Jesus that drove him to empty himself in dying for you unto the last drop of blood as he imaged the perfect love of the heavenly Father for you.

Baptism in the Holy Spirit

St. John writes that Jesus could not send the Spirit of love into your heart because he had not yet died (Jn

176 THE EVERLASTING NOW

7:39). Yet when Jesus does die and is risen to a new oneness in human form of imaging the love of the Father for every human person, he can pour into your heart the Father's Spirit. St. Paul could write that if the Spirit of Jesus raised him to new life, so the same Spirit can raise you into a sharing of his eternal, glorious life.

> . . . the Spirit of God has made his home in you. . . Though your body may be dead it is because of sin, but if Christ is in you then your spirit is life itself because you have been justified: and if the Spirit of him who raised Jesus from the dead is living in you, then he who raised Jesus from the dead will give life to your own mortal bodies through his Spirit living in you (Rom 8:9-11).

Through the Spirit of the risen Jesus living in you, you are made heirs with Christ and as you share in his sufferings so you also will share in his glory (Rom 8:16-17; Gal 4:6-7). You are thus able to share Jesus' very own life living within you because of his Spirit that he gives to you. This is why St. Paul does not always clearly distinguish the Spirit from the risen Jesus, for now the risen Lord cannot be experienced both as risen and as raising you to a share in dying to yourself and rising to a new life in him except through his Spirit. The repercussions of such an ontological change in your nature, now becoming, as St. John says, "God's children and that is what we are" (1 Jn 3:1), are endless as you strive to live according to this inner dignity. You are called out of darkness, sin and death into the light, holiness and life of Jesus risen and therefore you must put aside the works of darkness.

> Since you have been brought back to true life with Christ, you must look for the things that are in heaven, where Christ is, sitting at

God's right hand. Let your thoughts be on heavenly things, not on the things that are on the earth, because you have died, and now the life you have is hidden with Christ in God. But when Christ is revealed—and he is your life—you too will be revealed in your glory with him (Col 3:1-4).

Jesus Is Lord

St. Paul gives to the risen, glorified Jesus the title of Lord *(Kyrios* in Greek) to indicate that after the resurrection Jesus is truly one with Yahweh. Jesus now in glory possesses a messianic transcendence, an exercise of royal sovereignty and dominion over the entire cosmos and not merely over Christians. Certain modern, liberal theologians err who insist that the power of Jesus' resurrection consists, not in his continued consciousness in his glorious life, but only in our hope that if we now live, as he did, forgetting ourselves, we too shall find meaningfulness in this present life.[8]

The early church testified through the apostles who witnessed to Jesus' resurrection because they "saw" him, and they knew through the Holy Spirit received at Pentecost that this same Jesus was in glory and yet was still living in them and operating with all of his power so that they, too, could believe the good news that they were freed of their own selfishness to live for one another. The presence of the indwelling Jesus transformed them into a new creation. St. Paul could write: "I have been crucified with Christ, and I live now not with my own life but with the life of Christ who lives in me" (Gal 2:19-20).

The joyful news was that ". . . for anyone who is in Christ, there is a new creation; the old creation has gone, and now the new one is here" (2 Cor 5:17). Jesus and the Father have come and now live within each disciple.It is a strong tradition in the New Testament on every page that the early Christians knew Jesus was risen and living in full consciousness, capable of abiding within the disciples (Jn 15:1-8) and working through them to reconcile the entire universe to the Father.[9]

Jesus—Pantocrator

St. Paul especially develops the doctrine of the risen Jesus who in glory has been given dominion over all things in the heavens and on earth. ". . . for in him were created all things in heaven and on earth; everything visible and everything invisible . . . and all things (are) to be reconciled through him and for him, everything in heaven and everything on earth, when he made peace by his death on the cross" (Col 1:15-20).

But Jesus in glory, interceding for you at the right hand of the Father, is not "up there," as many Christians may draw a picture of the heavenly throne. The power of the Holy Spirit, raising Jesus Christ to a new transcendence, one with the Father in majesty, glory and power, is a power that places the risen Christ "inside" your material world. Because the resurrection of Jesus makes him transcendent, it also renders him totally immanent to your present, material world.

Jesus' resurrection must be viewed, not only as the cause of his glorification and exaltation in heaven, something that has happened to him as an individual person, but as the efficacious moving force within you and through you in the material cosmos. We usually ignore this aspect by thinking that his resurrection will be effective only at the end of the world when we will individually share in his resurrection. We also need to see his resurrectional presence and his intercessory power as a dynamic force within the material universe. By his new and glorious life, Jesus is the new Adam and Lord of the universe, capable by his new life of leading us and through us the whole cosmos to a share in glory.

Again Jesus, the Lord of the universe, completes the world by sending you his Holy Spirit who imparts the very "uncreated energies" of God. This makes you a child of God, capable of working with Jesus in suffering, and sharing in his glory through the union of all things in him. It is only man of all God's creatures on earth who, by reflecting in the depths of his consciousness, is capable of finding the connection between Christ risen and the rest of creation. J. Huby, the Pauline scholar, has well synthesized how Christ gathers up all things to give them their fullest meaning in himself:

> In Him all has been created as in a supreme center of unity, harmony and cohesion, which gives to the world its sense, its value, and therefore its reality. Or, to use another metaphor, He is the focus, the "meeting point" as Lightfoot puts it, where all the fibres and generative energies of the universe are organized and gathered together. Were someone to see the whole universe, past, present and future, in a single instantaneous glimpse, he would see all beings ontologically suspended from Christ, and completely unintelligible apart from Him.[10]

Our Resurrection

You can now understand how futile it would have been to discuss our resurrection before we understood clearly what the resurrection of Jesus Christ means. Now you can break away from viewing your resurrection as an objectified moment at the last moment of this world's material existence. You can discard picturing your soul as coming back into the same material body and becoming the informing source of a new, spiritualized person that is very much, in the words of St. Thomas Aquinas, the same as you were when you reached the age of 33!

You are now in a position to regard resurrection as a process of continued living out of what was symbolized in your baptism: of dying to your self-centeredness by the power of Jesus' Spirit living in you in order to live *in* Jesus Christ to the glory and praise of the Father.

This process of moving in this life from a "perishable" body to an "imperishable" one is developed by St. Paul as he attempts to answer, what he terms, "stupid questions" (1 Cor 15:36), asked by the Corinthians concerning how dead people will rise and what sort of body they will then have.

Meaning of Body

As scripture and the teaching of the church continually refer to our earthly bodies and our resurrected bodies at the end of the world,[11] we must understand how the writers of the New Testament, especially St. Paul, understood this important concept.

St. Paul, as we have seen, presents the biblical man as conceived by the Jewish people. He is composed of a body (*soma* in Greek) that is for all purposes the whole man as a psychophysical unity, a personality *ad extra*, in relation to the created, material world around him. Hence body-man is made up of the soul or *psyche* with all the emotions and passions that we call irascible and concupiscible, as well as the *sarx* or the flesh. The *pneuma* or spirit is the total man as viewed in his unique personality through a knowing relationship in love to God. Man is *this* individual person because God calls him by his personal name. Man becomes conscious of his own unique identity by relating in a love act to God as his ground of being. In the *soma* or body, man is in solidarity with the material world, with his environment. Man relates to the cosmic world through the body. Can we conceive of man as ever losing his body or his relation in solidarity to the material cosmos?

A modern author describes the Pauline concept of body:

> For Paul the body cannot be reduced simply to the material component of the animated being which is man. It is enough to read, for example, 1 Cor 6:13-7:4; 12:12-27; 15:35-44 to gain an idea of what the body is: it makes possible the human existence willed by God; it expresses the possibilities of man's life; it allows sexual union and commits the whole being that it is and represents; it is the human person in his entirety, his identification, his reality with all its activities, its values, it is not merely one element among many; the word "body" rather describes man in a definite situation, in relation to others, than reduced to himself alone, rather than placed in a dynamism which makes him live with others, expresses his existence with its possibilities and its brief span, rather than man considered as static. The body is man responsible for what he does, for how he lives; it is his entire situation, his totality, his personality.[12]

St. Paul fought early Christian philosophers, like Hymenaeus and Philetus (2 Tm 2:18), and St. Irenaeus in the second century faced Valentinian Gnostics precisely because both groups relegated the resurrection merely to a *now* spiritual resurrection, denying that the materiality of man's bodily existence would also share in the resurrection. Paul and the early Christian apologists preached and wrote in defense of a general resurrection. But they also taught that such a fullness *in* Christ was preceded even now in this life by a share in Christ's resurrectional life.

Already Risen

Dominican theologian Pierre Benoit traces through St. Paul's growth in understanding how our human resurrection is a process that begins in baptism, is experienced immediately after death by those who have lived and died in Christ and will reach a fullness when the resurrection of Jesus, the Head, will be extended to all his followers and through them to the entire, material cosmos.[13]

Only in his letters (Ephesians and Colossians), written from his Roman prison, does Paul finally teach that even in this life we share in Christ's resurrection. In baptism we Christians are buried with Christ and "by baptism, too, you have been raised up with him through your belief in the power of God who raised him from the dead" (Col 2:12). By taking away our sins and bringing us to life with Christ, God "raised us up with him and gave us a place with him in heaven, in Christ Jesus" (Eph 2:5-6).

This new life in Christ is already yours in baptism and grows each time you "put on Christ" by dying to selfishness and rising to a new oneness in him. This new life is "not yet" in its fullness. Your bodily life, your total personhood, is still in the process of being baptized at each moment in Christ. This life is hidden with Christ in God and will only appear with the manifestation of the fullness of Christ in his *Parousia* (second coming).

Benoit summarizes Paul's thought:

> But he (Paul) gives the impression that while he abided by the traditional affirmation of the last resurrection, he regards it as less and less important and believes that the essential has already come to pass. His eschatology, which at the outset was "futurist," has become increasingly one that has already been effected.[14]

Eternal Life Even Now

The Johannine Gospel consistently presents the Good News as eternal life already given to the disciples of Jesus who keep his commandments and eat his body. Eternal life is already possessed by those who listen to his words and believe in the one who sent Jesus (Jn 5:24). It is the Father's will to raise up anyone who believes in the Son, and that person already possesses eternal life (Jn 6:40,47). Jesus' strongest statement, recorded by John in his Gospel, emphasizes that eternal life is already possessed by those who will never die despite their physical death.

> I am the resurrection.
> If anyone believes in me, even though he dies he
>   will live,
> and whoever lives and believes in me
> will never die.
> Do you believe this? (Jn 11:25-26).

The *eschaton* or the end of time in which you will receive the fullness of resurrection is already here as you believe in Christ and keep his teachings of dying to selfishness and rising to new self-giving, loving service toward others as he did.

Therefore, from the New Testament teachings are we not justified in seeing the resurrection of the body in a new way, no longer as a reanimation of the body through the return at the end of time of the soul into the dead body in the grave? Can we not view it as a process, having already begun among those justified in Christ by a conscious living of their baptism, and repeated in a commitment of growing intensity when they in their *pneuma* or spirit die to any autonomy of self-love, rooted in the flesh and the passions, and yield to the everlasting *now* of the love of God always present to them? Your resurrection thus becomes an *evolving event*, not in the historical sequence of *chronos*, as a static moment at the end of the world, but in the spiritual determination of conscious love that theologians call *kairos,* God's time, salvation-time, in which you opt to become truly human by answering to God's call within you. In this sense, the *soma,* with its body relation of ourselves to the cosmos, rises into a higher participation of the life of the spirit. Your *soma* or body relationships become integrated with your *pneuma* or spirit relationships so that, as a total person you experience the world in God and God in the world.

A Resurrected Body

We believe that Jesus broke through the limitations of our human confinement to attain total enlightenment and perfect, loving presence to the entire universe in his resurrection and exaltation. He allowed his early disciples a glimpse into his resurrectional presence. He came to them through closed doors, came upon some as they were walking. His body assumed different forms so they only gradually recognized him in the breaking of the bread or through some other manifestation. As he could suddenly appear, so he could suddenly disappear.

St. Paul tried to hold on to the process of the *already* and the *not yet* of the resurrection as experienced by us humans. He taught that the whole person in Christ in this life would be raised up and given a glorious body. The body, again in his thinking, is not a part, but the whole person, individuated and recognized in his or her unique personality, sharing in some mysterious way that Paul does not think important or even possible to describe. He writes that Jesus will transfigure these poor bodies of ours into "copies of his glorious body" (Phil 3:21).

In the resurrection of the dead, "the thing that is sown is perishable but what is raised is imperishable; the thing that is sown is contemptible but what is raised is glorious; the thing that is sown is weak but what is raised is powerful; when it is sown, it embodies the soul, when it is raised it embodies the spirit" (1 Cor 15:42-44). Your glorified being will nevermore suffer or die. Your risen body will enjoy a brilliance reflecting the spiritual wisdom you reached in faith, hope and love on earth. St. Paul admits that we cannot ponder with our human reasoning what awaits us (1 Cor 2:9). Yet Holy Scripture gives us analogies. "The Lord God will be shining on them. . . . We shall be like Him because we shall see Him as He really is" (Rv 22:5 and 1 Jn 3:2). Daniel said: "The learned will shine as brightly as the vault of heaven and those who have instructed many in virtue, as bright as stars for all eternity" (Dn 12:3).

Those in Glory

Can we not hold what the church has constantly taught, that those who die in Christ and have been sufficiently healed of all traces of selfishness from their earthly existence, even now receive a share in glory and hence are already risen? Does this not follow in seeing resurrection as a process, a degree of being one in Christ, of being divinized as a child of God and living already in the risen Christ, whose resurrectional body is a part of those who are one with him, their Head?

If the saints are already in glory and exist in the state called heaven, are they not united intimately with the risen Jesus? The beautiful dogma of Mary's Assumption into heaven declares that she, the archetype of the heavenly church, already exists in heaven with a glorified body. The definition is couched in terms of Mary's body and soul: "We proclaim and define it to be a dogma revealed by God that the immaculate mother of God, Mary ever Virgin, when the course of her earthly life was finished, was taken up" body and soul to heavenly glory.[15]

Mary is described in Vatican II's *Constitution on the Church:* "The mother of Jesus, in the glory which she possesses body and soul in heaven, is the image and beginning of the Church as it is to be perfected in the world to come" (no. 68). If the saints are also in glory, forming the Church Triumphant along with Mary, could we not argue with Irish theologian Donal Flanagan[16] that she is a type of the Pilgrim Church but is a part of the Triumphant Church wherein she and the other saints, already sharing in the glory of the risen Lord, participate in a glorious way in his resurrection?

Final Glory

Holy Scripture and the church have never fluctuated in the teaching about an end of our historical time and with that a glorification, not only of those who have lived intimately through the Holy Spirit in the Body of Christ but of the entire, created universe. Just as the doctrine of the risen Jesus describes how divinity and humanity came together in a oneness of person, so the church teaches that God has created the entire world, each atom of matter, each individual human being and each angel, all to become a vital part of that one Body of Christ. All creatures will share his eternal, trinitarian life by being a part of that Body. And that Body will be the source of praise and glory to him, the source of all life and beauty.

We pilgrims in the church of Christ, his Body Militant, are still growing into the "utter fullness of God" (Eph 3:19). Jesus Christ lives in each of us. Our growth in the love of Christ comes from, through and with him. Each member of his Body must continue to open up to that presence of Jesus within and to Jesus present outside, in the lives of all men, guiding the whole world into the final completion. Each of us, with St. Paul after Damascus, must eagerly seek to find Jesus present as an immanent force, actively working, suffering, rejoicing in his members as his whole Body grows in and through the created world.

All of us have a unique role to play in reconciling the

world that is still groaning in travail before it is brought to full life in Christ (Rom 8:22-23). The resurrected Body of Christ is being raised now as we learn to surrender ourselves in loving service to each other through his Holy Spirit. The housewife, teacher, policeman, office worker, farmer, religious or lay man or woman, all must live consciously in Christ a life of constant response to his Lordship as he speaks God's presence in his Word in each moment of their lives.

The resurrection of the full Christ comes in death, in the cross, a symbol of continued purification and conversion away from the dark egoism to the inner light of Jesus within us. Resurrection is a series of saying "yes" to the dictates of Jesus' Spirit. Thus we become "reconcilers." God gave us this work of handing on this reconciliation (2 Cor 5:18). We have the dignity, by our service (*diakonia* in Greek) within the Body of Christ, to extend the reconciliation by Christ of all things back to his Father.

Jesus is not only the Alpha (Jn 1:2) but he is now, through his members in his Body the church, Militant and Triumphant and Suffering, inserted into the cosmos and is bringing the material world to its fullness. He is also the Omega, the goal, the end toward which every creature is being drawn as by a magnetic force of personal love.

The Second Coming

Christian doctrine teaches us that Christ will come at the end of time to transform this universe by bringing it to its completion in and through himself.

> And when everything is subjected to him, then the Son himself will be subject in this turn to the One who subjected all things to him, so that God may be all in all (1 Cor 15:28).

Our Christian faith believes that Jesus will complete

his work, which began after his death and resurrection, continued through his glorious risen life, and lives within the members of his Body, the church. But in a real sense the *Parousia* (Greek word for *presence,* implying the arrival of a person) has already happened since Jesus Christ in his resurrectional life has been present unceasingly. It is not so much another epiphany, the coming of Christ from outside into our world as in the incarnation, that we await but the fullness of his "diaphany," to use Teilhard de Chardin's term, the "shining through" matter of the living presence of Jesus risen.

Jesus is present and is now bringing about the victory over the dark powers of cosmic evil. But in a true sense his victory will be perfect only at the end of time and this is the usual sense in which we use the term *Parousia.* It is a gradual transformation, not a destruction, of God's creation. The *Parousia* will come when the Gospel will have been preached to the entire universe. It is rooted in Christian hope and testifies that Christian redemption includes not merely the spiritual side of mankind, but embraces also the materiality of the whole cosmos. But the Good News is that Jesus Christ is already here bringing about the kingdom of heaven in our lives and through us in the whole world.

A great temptation for pious Christians is to fall into the trap of taking literally the scriptural images of life after death as though they will happen in human history as our minds understand the pictures given to us to describe mysteries that cannot be comprehended in this life. To be concerned about what kind of heaven awaits us, what kind of body we will have, what joys will be ours in heaven, to believe we have already been saved so now we have merely to wait for that great day when Jesus will come in a cloud of glory to snatch us up with him to live forever in glory. . . these can distract us from the true message of Jesus and his true reality in our present regard.

Joseph Bonsirven, a noted New Testament scholar, describes the eschatological message of the Gospels:

> The doctrine of the resurrection of the body on the last day is retained, but there is no description of the *Parousia,* or of the signs which will precede the Second Coming. Instead, the emphasis is placed on the element of present fulfillment: eternal life is present possession, the spiritual is already given to us; the Judgment itself is anticipated in the present and so is the *Parousia.*[17]

Conclusion

Today you, like most human beings, are surrounded by a world that is at each moment exploding into new riches. You are searching for meaningfulness amid so much multiplicity. You look for a center where there is peace, even though, around the center, cyclone winds blow fiercely. One of the newest temptations today is to offer cheap meaningfulness to human beings in the form of innumerable seminars, institutes, books and do-it-yourself gimmicks to expand consciousness. And when you seriously do take the courage to extend your consciousness beyond your immediate needs to ask what is ultimate meaningfulness for you in terms of what comes after final death, you receive two answers. Parapsychologists show you the wonders of psychic powers. Your present, future and ultimate future consist, they tell you, in developing such powers of mental telepathy, precognition, psychokinesis and all the other ESP abilities. Your happiness will consist in living on such high levels of expanded consciousness through the continued development of your psychic energies.

The other answer you receive from formal religions. Being a Christian, you are taught to look forward to a heaven. You will enter heaven after the final resurrection when your soul has returned to your risen body to enjoy an eternal beatific vision of God. You will meet all your friends and be able to travel quickly to any part of the universe, even to presently unexplored planets.[18] There will be no pain, but only all the joys you ever had on earth, yet infinitely more enjoyable. Death is painted as a "sweet" reunion with your loved ones and, therefore, must not be feared. Troubles of this earthly existence can be endured stoically because there is an immortal life of unending pleasures awaiting you.

The danger is such a view of life after death is that it can be loaded with selfishness and completely distorts the message of Jesus and his early followers. One writer rebukes such persons who selfishly want to continue forever their same self-centered world as lived on this earth.

> The belief in my own eternity seems to me in-deed to be a piece of unwarranted self-glorification, and the desire for it a gross con-cession to selfishness.[19]

Jesus, as well as St. Paul and the other early Christians, taught a hope in the resurrection that veered away from anything that would place human hope in man himself or in material things. We saw already how Jesus promised eternal life but only for those who kept his word. The seed had to fall into the earth and die before it could bring forth new fruit. He was not concerned with details about the end of the world. He was concerned with teaching people how to live totally for God and for one another. St. Paul branded all speculative questions about the life to come, especially about our resurrected bodies, as "stupid questions" (1 Cor 15:36).

Jurgen Moltmann calls us back to our responsibility to live dynamically in this present world through self-sacrifice for others.

This means, however, that the hope of resurrection must bring about a new understanding of the world. This world is not the heaven of self-realization, as it was said to be in Idealism. This world is not the hell of self-estrangement, as it is said to be in romanticist and existentialist writing. The world is not yet finished, but is understood as engaged in a history. It is therefore the world of possibilities, the world in which we can serve the future, promised truth and righteousness and peace. This is an age of diaspora, of sowing in hope, of self-surrender and sacrifice, for it is an age which stands within the horizon of a new future. Thus self-expenditure in this world, day-to-day love in hope, becomes possible and becomes human within that horizon of expectation which transcends this world. The glory of self-realization and the misery of self-estrangement alike arise from hopelessness in a world of lost horizons. To disclose to it the horizon of the future of the crucified Christ is the task of the Christian Church.[20]

The true message of the resurrection lies in your readiness to listen to Christ's teaching about the cross and death in loving self-sacrifice for others and to live that teaching. To consider the resurrection or any part of the world to come in terms solely of your own personal immortality can all too easily be a cop-out for extending selfish immaturity into eternity. True human maturity consists in your ability to live for the entire cosmos, to strive to use your present life to develop this God-given world into a world according to his mind by self-sacrificing love for others.

The teaching of Jesus and his own human growth process touch powerfully on the cross, death and resurrection as interrelated factors in moving him from earthly existence to his glorious resurrection. He was raised in glory by his Father because he lived totally for him. His every thought was centered on pleasing his Father. But such a life of love to please his Father at all times by being the image of the self-emptying love of his Father for each and every human person was a call to die to his own self-centeredness. Because Jesus died to himself and sought meaningfulness in fulfilling God's purpose for the entire universe by loving each of us unto death, God raised him in glory. Our resurrection will come about, is *now* happening, in the same way.

Jesus insists that if you want to be his disciple and obtain eternal life you have to begin by a "dying" process. You have to enter into a suffering, but such that would deliver you unto new life. You have to take the risk of surrendering yourself to him by giving up lower levels of self-absorption which allow you to dominate and control your own life, and to accept Christ's invitation to move onto a higher level of existence by being guided in love by his Holy Spirit. Suffering and dying, the cross, are only stepping-stones to a new life, to the ongoing process of resurrection.

> If anyone wants to be a follower of mine, let him renounce himself and take up his cross and follow me. For anyone who wants to save his life will lose it; but anyone who loses his life for my sake will find it (Mt 16:24-25).

Your hope is in the resurrection of Christ, that, as he lived for his heavenly Father and for you and not for himself and was glorified, so you also must live for others with the love of Jesus, his Spirit, living in you and giving you the power to be love toward all. Your hope for heaven is a continued growth in forgetting yourself in order to let God's love within you shine out to all you meet. At the heart of your resurrection and your eternal life in heaven is your present hope that in suffering with Christ in this life of loving service toward others, your dying will bring you into new, transforming life.

It means that, as you freely consent to accept sufferings and the cross, as you enter into the darkness of each human situation, bound up by so much sin, absurdity and meaninglessness, you hope beyond all hope that you, too, will share in Jesus' eternal life. You are "sharing his sufferings so as to share his glory" (Rom 8:17). "If we have died with him, then we shall live with him. If we hold firm, then we shall reign with him" (2 Tm 2:11-12).

Into the dark silence of our world the brightness of the risen Jesus enters. He who was light from all eternity consented to take into his brightness the darkness of a human consciousness and an unconscious. He grew into complete resurrectional brightness and glory by accepting the darkness of temptations, above all, the greatest, to hold onto his life or to lose it out of love for his Father on our behalf. Through obedience he brought his human consciousness and unconscious into a wholeness. By dying to self and living in love for each one of us, he grew into the glorious image of his heavenly Father.

And now his brightness is given to you and me that we might be led from the darkness of selfishness into the light of loving service for others. We have seen his glory in hope. But it is still night. We cry out in hope: "Come, Lord Jesus. *Marana tha!*" (Rv 22:20).

I guess this is why I like butterflies. But more and more the dark caterpillar is also becoming my friend. For the Good News of Jesus is that the caterpillar is the butterfly! Hope in the transformation of what will come to be passes through the cocoon of doubt and fear, darkness and absurdity. It leads to the realization that there is only *one* Butterfly and he is Christ. We are now fashioning his beautiful body. We even now know: "There is only Christ: he is everything and he is in everything" (Col 3:11).

But we hope for that eternal life where, through God's Spirit of love, we will praise the Father forever in the oneness of Jesus Christ in whose image we have been created. In that oneness with Christ we will learn to love all beings in him. His resurrectional love will permeate us as it has in this life, giving us a sense of the inner beauty and uniqueness of each other person, as we lovingly share our uniqueness of God's beauty in us. The true message of eternal life is that of love. Jesus in human form lived out what is at the heart of the triune God and of the essence of heaven: an *I-Thou* in self-sacrificing love of a *We* community. Greater love experienced begets a greater readiness to die to isolation and to live for the entire community, the Body of Christ. There is only Christ! He is everything! And he is in everything!

> And we, with our unveiled faces reflecting like mirrors the brightness of the Lord, all grow brighter and brighter as we are turned into the image that we reflect; this is the work of the Lord who is Spirit (2 Cor 3:18).

Appendices

Appendix One
Whatever Happened to Limbo?

In previous chapters we have touched on the states of heaven, hell and purgatory. Such states after death apply to adults who, during life on earth, freely opted in some way or other to love God and neighbor. But down through the centuries Christians have asked what happens to children who have not been baptized and have not been given the opportunities to develop their intellectual and volitional powers. Since the beginning of the human race this number must be astronomical. In our modern age this problem becomes poignant in the face of so many millions of abortions performed annually.

Theologians are placed in a quandary due to scriptural revelation and the traditional teachings of the church. Scripture assures us that God has created all of us according to his own image (Gn 1:26). He wishes all human beings to be saved, i.e., to share in his eternal life. "He (God) wants everyone to be saved and reach full knowledge of the truth" (1 Tm 2:4). Jesus Christ died for every human being that he or she may have eternal life.

And yet, as the church teaches, Jesus insisted that one had to be reborn by water and the Spirit (Jn 3:5). To be saved one had to profess that Jesus is Lord. "By believing from the heart you are made righteous; by confessing with your lips you are saved" (Rom 10:10).

How can children, who die before receiving baptism, before having a chance to develop a general desire to love God, ever reach salvation?

Various Solutions

Over the centuries Christian theologians have proposed theories about the fate of such children. One early attempt at a solution that occasionally reappears even in modern times is that of *Universalism*. This, basically, is an optimism that places complete faith in God's power and merciful love to carry through with his salvific will. Ultimately, it assures us, hell and any other place or state of confinement will give way and only heaven will exist for all eternity. In a word, eventually all human beings will be saved. The problem of children dying in original sin without baptism becomes, therefore, no problem. Origen's theory of *apokatastasis*, or the universal recapitulation of all human beings to God in eternal salvation with the final dissolution of hell, has been condemned by the Second Ecumenical Council of Constantinople in 553.

St. Augustine agonized over the destiny of such children. Yet he could not reconcile Jesus' ultimate verdict that in the Last Judgment there would be only heaven or hell (Mt 25:31-46) with the Pelagian teaching that infants dying without baptism went to limbo. Limbo (from the late Latin word *limbus*, meaning hem or border) is the theological term applied to the place or state where those who died before Christ's redemption temporarily waited for deliverance *(limbus patrum)*, or the permanent place or state where children who die without baptism are deprived of the beatific vision.

We find Augustine writing to St. Jerome: "When the question of the punishment of children is raised, it troubles me sorely, I assure you, and I am at a loss what to answer." His thinking, however, became quite definite in his later years. Many theologians in the Middle Ages and in the period of Jansenism held his same view, namely, that such infants, because they possess original sin on their souls, cannot be in heaven. Therefore, they must ultimately be found in hell. He does concede, however, that their punishment in hell would mean the lack of the beatific vision and would be of the mildest kind.[1]

The majority of theologians followed St. Thomas Aquinas and St. Anselm of Canterbury in viewing limbo as the state in which unbaptized infants will not see God in the beatific vision. However, they will not be in hell but in a natural state of happiness that would allow them to experience enjoyment of all the natural goods that they possess.

The Magisterium of the Church

It must be recognized that the teaching about limbo has never been clearly defined in any church document. Limbo is one theological speculation of what happens to children who die without baptism. Pope Innocent III in 1201 wrote to the Archbishop of Arles that actual sin is punished by the endless torment of hell, but original sin is punished by the loss of the vision of God.[2] The ecumenical councils of Lyons II and Florence defined that souls that die in mortal sin or with original sin alone go down into hell to receive differing punishments.[3] But this does not seem to be a statement about limbo.

The Council of Trent defined that all human beings are born in the state of original sin and that this sin is removed by baptism, either actual or by desire.[4] But it is clearly not a statement that there is anyone who died in original sin alone. Thus the stance of the official teaching church has been one of neither approving nor rejecting the doctrine of limbo.

New Approaches

Theologians in the last few decades have developed new theories that aim at taking the abrasive edge off the Augustinian view or even the "natural end" view of the traditional teaching of theologians on limbo. George Dyer gives a review of these latest theories.[5]

M. Laurenge appeals to God's sincere salvific will as powerful enough to find some way that such a child, dying without baptism, would find the necessary means of salvation after death. He argues for an awakening of the child's powers to know God after death. In this knowledge the child would be given a choice for or against God as its final goal. Depending on this free choice, it would enter into the state of heaven or hell for all eternity.[6]

Vincent Wilkins, S.J., allows for the child after death to remain in the state of limbo until the general resurrection when such a child comes forth and is reborn to the supernatural life in Christ and enters into eternal heaven.[7] At the end of the world such children issue from limbo as fully grown adults, ready for heaven. His theory maintains that in the final judgment there are only adults.

In earlier chapters we have pointed out the theory of many modern theologians, called the *final option*. When this is applied to the problem of infants dying without baptism and the question of limbo, according to P. Glorieux[8] and L. Boros[9], children are given an opportunity at the very moment of death to know God and Jesus Christ, and in that moment to make a final and decisive option for or against God. Thus God's salvific will is truly preserved in granting to all human beings, while in this earthly existence, the opportunity to know God sufficiently to freely choose God over self. This does not mean that all children reaching such maturity in the last moment of life will choose God.

A Mystery

What can be said about these attempts to pierce the mystery of what happens to children who die without baptism? These are all attempts that may, on the one side preserve a revealed truth, but from another side may be a bit weak and inadequate, even eclipsing another truth.

In any theory, however, there are three truths that must be kept in mind.

The first is that God is love and that he has freely created all human beings, including children, in order that they may all share in his eternal happiness, that they may come to know and love him. In this present order of economy God works through his visible church and the sacraments to mediate himself as gift in love to all human beings and, therefore, he seems to "need" other human beings on this earth to bring others to him. Nevertheless, we must believe that his universal, salvific will can work, not only in this earthly existence but also in the life to come, in a way that befits his infinite mercy and love.

Second, we must hold that Jesus died on the cross to save all human beings, including children. He is the eternal High Priest who is always interceding not only for the human race, but for each individual in particular.

Third, we know that, as was pointed out in the chapter on hell, we are condemned to such punishments not so much by God's vindictive decrees but by individual, self-centered choices made during our lifetime. We enter into eternal existence with the type of consciousness that we formed in our earthly relationships toward God, others and ourself. Therefore, we can safely believe that no one will be deprived of God who has not freely turned away through sins personally committed.

St. Augustine and his followers viewed original sin as a static "thing" inherited by being human. It was like a little black spot on the human soul. If a child died without baptism, it had to suffer the consequences. An obstacle prevented such a person from "seeing" God and enjoying his presence for all eternity.

A loving society is important to the reestablishment of individuals who through lack of love have been deprived of full human growth. How can we then doubt that the fate of millions of unbaptized children will rest in the infinite love of God the Father?

It will always remain a mystery to us how loving Christians can meet the underdeveloped human beings after their death and bring the experience of God's infinite love to them.

Why should we not learn to trust in God when our intellects have reached a limit in solving possible problems? One thing we can be absolutely certain of: God is love. His loving mercy endures forever. What is impossible to man is possible to God.

Appendix Two
Out-of-the-Body Experiences

In 1975 Dr. Raymond Moody published *Life After Life*, which became an immediate best-seller.[1] Several million people read his book or saw the popular movie version entitled, *Beyond and Back,* produced by Sunn Classic Pictures. Dr. Elisabeth Kubler-Ross, through her two books[2] and her innumerable lectures and interviews around the country, has also brought to public attention some of the phenomena that occur when people have a near-death experience. Even though the medical world may define such occurrences as "clinical deaths," they must be considered as pseudo deaths, since the persons really do not die but are resuscitated by various means.

Such writings are not new. The 8th-century classic, *The Tibetan Book of the Dead,*[3] describes near-death experiences with details that parallel the cases described by Moody and Kubler-Ross. Carl G. Jung, along with many other psychologists, and writers, such as Edgar Allen Poe, give similar descriptions to persons experiencing death, but living through it to describe the details.[4] Much more detailed work has been done by Dr. Karlis Osis and Dr. E. Haraldsson, who have scientifically examined the observations of physicians and nurses who assisted in over a thousand cases at either actual deaths with no return or near-death experiences.[5]

What is new in the findings of such researchers as Moody, Kubler-Ross and Osis is their definite assertion of life after death. They describe death as a transition into a new life that usually brings great peace and joy to the one undergoing the experience. Becoming acquainted with such experiences, argue these writers, we can better prepare those who are dying. We can better live now, knowing that death is not an end but a passing into a new existence.

Thus in the '70s death has suddenly become not only popular but even an exciting topic. Classes are offered for the young in high schools and for senior citizens. Thanatology is an approved branch of psychology and medicine that trains specialists in the process of dying and how to prepare those who are about to undergo death.

In dealing with such a topic we must clearly distinguish between two distinct experiences of death. There is the "complete" death, with no return. Dr. K. Osis has done the most up-to-date research on what such dying persons have undergone in death, as recorded by physicians and nurses who worked with the terminally ill. Then there are the more popular and intriguing accounts of those who enter into a pseudo death or have a near-death experience. Such persons themselves later are able to relate to us, through researchers like Moody and Kubler-Ross, what they experience. It is this last type that stirs up most interest since such experiences are being told by the eyewitnesses themselves.

Certain common elements seem to emerge in such near-death experiences. One common experience is that of a transcendence, lifting up the person into a foreign region or dimension of great light and beauty, or a series of autoscopic experiences, namely, a self-visualization from a position of height. In such experiences there is a "floating" sensation that has been commonly described as being "out of the body." While detached from the physical body, but still maintaining some "etheric" or "aural" body, such persons observe their very own body in clear detail as well as nearby objects, persons around an operating table, and various machines that normally are out of the range of vision of the body on the operating table.

One patient described this in the following words: "It was like sitting up in a balcony looking down at a movie."[6] Amidst all such visions of persons and things, there is a sense of deep peace and joyfulness. Dr. Moody relates that in the cases which he researched the persons heard rumbling sounds; they seemed to have been drawn out of their bodies through a tunnel. They often met apparitions of the dead or some guide, a "being of light"; and usually they returned to life with a new perspective, no longer fearing death.

Pseudo-death Experiences

A decade before Moody's work, Dr. Robert Crookall, a British geologist, had been publishing detailed studies of near-death and other out-of-the-body experiences. He pointed out that many persons report having had out-of-the-body experiences (OBEs) without having a near-death experience.[7] In his works, Dr. Crookall points out that pseudo-death experiences and conventional OBEs are virtually the same phenomenon.

Just what is an out-of-the-body experience? It is a phenomenon that occurs more commonly than is believed. Persons who have perfected a trance state, such as Edgar Cacey and Robert Monroe,[8] through self-hypnosis or relaxation techniques have been able at will to project their "soul" out of their body so that the thinking self can be removed, at least in an impression, from the body. They seemingly are capable of seeing the body in one place and the thinking self detached and found locally in another. What seems most interesting about such experiences, especially as recorded by those who have clinically died and returned after resuscitation, is that the thinking consciousness of man is never really separated from a body. In such an out-of-the-body experience, the "person" is seen clothed with an *auric* or *etheric* body, thus still localizing the person, so that a human being seems never to be a pure spirit without reference to an informed body.[9]

This opens us up to many intriguing questions. Do pseudo deaths and the visions recorded by those who truly die really prove to us that we will survive with a consciousness after death? Are such experiences psychically produced or are they merely psychological phenomena with no true objectivity? What can be said to be the cause of out-of-the-body experiences? Those who preach religion, especially Christianity, and parapsychologists with some more recent psychologists, such as Kubler-Ross and Moody, tend to believe that such experiences are a real psychic "happening" and indicate a survival of life after death. Some other psychologists have been exploring the psychological dimension and are busy formulating theories that explain such happenings as psychological reactions to stressful, anxiety-laden situations.

What do such experiences have to tell Christians? Dr. Malachi B. Martin sounds a rather somber note of caution to such scientific researchers. Besides claiming that often they go beyond the facts in taking a special sampling and making universal statements that should apply to all persons as they similarly enter into a death experience, he warns:

Psychiatrists would be well advised to avoid entanglements in an area where they have no competence, and where the results of unprofessional intervention are dire. Among the saddest cases a professional exorcist undertakes is to help psychiatrists or psychologists who have ventured beyond their professional limits and fallen afoul of forces they did not suspect existed, and whose cunning they could not fathom. . . . At best the message of those chosen as subjects by the thanatologists is useless as proof of a future life.[10]

Deathbed Visions

First, we might ask, Do the visions that persons on their deathbed "see"—visions of their dead loved ones, of angels, Christ, the saints or other mythical, religious figures—give us proof of a survival after death? Does it mean that such persons, as they die, really are in contact with spiritualized persons from another life? Dr. Osis and other such researchers seem to think that these visions are not explainable by psychological factors creating them but that they are true psychic experiences of an objective order. Their reason for such a statement is tied to the fact that many times the person seeing such visions is not aware of his or her imminent death. At other times there were visions of persons who had died but their death was unknown to the persons receiving the visions.

Researcher D. Scott Rogo, however, holds that such deathbed visions are basically psychological manifestations. "There is now a growing amount of clinical evidence at hand indicating that a person, even though he does not consciously realize that he is dying, keeps unconscious tabs on his physical state. A terminally ill patient may very well know, at a deeply unconscious level, exactly when he or she will die. I don't consider it unlikely that a dying person might unconsciously project visions of the dead coming to greet him. This might be a mechanism the mind uses to alleviate anxiety."[11]

Return to Life After Death

Tied to deathbed visions is the out-of-body experience, whereby an individual returns to life from what seemed to be a true death. Perhaps we can look at a psychological explanation similar to the one offered for deathbed visions, in order to see if persons experiencing a "near-death" really had a true separation from the material body, or if they had a psychological "impression," or some other psychological means of interpreting what seemed to happen.

Researchers have been quick to point out, in order to establish the objectivity of out-of-body experiences, that there are accompanying psychic phenomena such as extrasensory perception, psychokinesis (the ability to move material objects with the mind) or visions.

The question comes down to this: Is it necessary to assume some form of mind-body separation to account for the psychological and parapsychological data that have been accumulated in research on near-death OBEs?

Dr. John Palmer develops an intriguing theory to explain such happenings on sheer psychological grounds.[12] Using Freudian terminology, Palmer's hypothesis is that the OBE is triggered by a more or less distinct change in the person's body concept. This change in identity comes usually through physical or psychological stress caused by such things as illness, fever, surgery, migraine headaches, accidents and emotional strain.

This theory maintains that the change in body image produces a basic psychological threat to the person's sense of individual identity, and this threat he seeks to resolve in part through the vehicle of "primary-process" imagery. Often the person may not be fully conscious of the threat or at least of the change of body image in the case of a strong anxiety attack. The unconscious mind must convince the ego of the "truth" of the new identity if the threat is to be alleviated. Palmer gives us the important tie-up with near-death experiences. In both Western and many non-Western cultures, death is interpreted in the dominant traditions as a separation of the soul from the body. "Whether or not a dying person accepts this particular teaching intellectually, the possibility of immortality and of the soul leaving the body is bound to be on his mind."[13]

The advantage of such a psychological explanation of OBE and near-death experiences is that it does not presuppose what it is trying to explain, namely, it does not require a mind-body separation. The other usual explanation of psychic phenomena revealing a supposedly objective body-soul separation seems to posit that as a theory. It ends up trying to prove its basic beginning point, that persons having a body-soul separation experience, could be programming themselves to such an experience by the unconscious having already accepted this as the objective way we are constituted in life after death.

Meaning of It All

Much more research must be done by psychologists and parapsychologists before we can have strong evidence that the psychic phenomena which accompany out-of-the-body experiences, especially in pseudo-death experiences, really do prove a survival of conscious personality after death. Two things can be said in conclusion to all the facts presented in this appendix on OBE. The first is a caution that the research done by Drs. Osis, Kubler-Ross, Moody and so many other psychologists and parapsychologists, not be accepted as definite proof of survival after death. The second, also a caution, is that, above all, we do not allow the attractive, psychic phenomena, desired by all of us naturally, which are described as part of the OBE, to lull us into an unreal and naive thinking that death then will always be exciting.

Death is a horrendous happening. It happens to the whole person and not merely to the body. I can be led, in reading such descriptions of death, to see death as a step to new, natural powers and not to an entrance to a new and eternal life that is predicated on the decisions of my earthly life. I can put off living dynamically this present moment because death only promises more "natural" power than I now have.

This leads to the other conclusion. Whatever psychologists and parapsychologists tell us about the phenomena that accompany those who truly die (and hence do not return) and those who have a pseudo-death experience, we will never have absolute certainty that when *I* die, I will survive after death. Only one man, Jesus Christ, died completely and returned to tell us through sharing with us the power of his resurrection that, if we live now in the dying process of forgetting self and loving others, we will live forever. This will always necessitate an act of humble faith. But this will yield to us a certainty also. It will not be the absolute certainty that science habitually strives to give that we will survive with greater self-powers. But it will be true certitude that becomes more certain as we experience in each present moment the passing over from our false self-containment to enter into a union with God and neighbor and the whole cosmic order by our readiness to love and humbly serve others.

Science may confirm what religious faith has already taught us: Death is a separation, but from selfishness. New life in survival is measured not by psychic phenomena but by loving oneness with God and his created universe.

I am the resurrection.
If anyone believes in me, even though he dies he
   will live,
and whoever lives and believes in me
will never die.
Do you believe this? (Jn 11:25-26).

Footnotes

Introduction

1. J.P. Sartre, *Nausea* (N.Y.: New Directions, 1964) p. 112.
2. Dr. Rollo May as cited by Gladys M. Hunt, *Don't Be Afraid to Die* (Grand Rapids, Mich.: Zondervan, 1971) pp. 17-18.
3. Ortega Y Gasset Jose, *Revolt of the Masses* (N.Y.: W.W. Norton & Co. 1932) p. 157.

Chapter One

1. Carlos Castaneda, *Journey to Ixtlan* (N.Y.: Simon and Schuster, 1972) pp. 108, 111.
2. A. Toynbee et al., *Man's Concern with Death* (N.Y.: McGraw-Hill, 1969) p. 131.
3. Sophocles, *Oedipus at Colonus*, pp. 1224-1226 in *Tragedies* (Chicago: Chicago Univ. Press).
4. Lucretius, *De Rerum Natura*, Bk. III, pp. 830-831, tr. H.A.J. Munro (4th ed. 1954-1957, Vol. 1, London; G. Bell & Sons, 1898-1900).
5. Richard W. Doss, *The Last Enemy* (N.Y.: Harper & Row, Publishers, 1974) p. 50.

Chapter Two

1. Karl Rahner, S.J., *On the Theology of Death* (N.Y.: Herder & Herder, 1961), tr. Charles H. Henkey.
2. *Ibid.*, p. 30.
3. Cf. Paul Chauchard, *Man and Cosmos* (N.Y.: Herder & Herder, 1965) tr. George Courtright, p. 143. Jose-Maria Gonzalez-Ruiz, "Should We De-Mythologize the Separated Soul?" in *Concilium*, Vol. 41, *Dogma, the Problem of Eschatology* (N.Y.: Paulist Press, 1969) pp. 82-96; also Anton Grabner-Haider, "The Biblical Understanding of 'Resurrection' and 'Glorification' " *ibid.*, pp. 66-81.

4. Rahner, *ibid.*, pp. 93-94.

5. E. Kubler-Ross, *On Death and Dying* (N.Y.: Macmillan Company, 1969) pp. 34 ff.

6. E. Kubler-Ross, *On Death and Dying.* Also *Questions and Answers on Death and Dying* (N.Y.: Macmillan Company, 1974); *Death: The Final Stage of Growth* (Englewood Cliffs, N.J.: Prentice-Hall, Inc., 1975).

7. R.A. Moody, *Life After Life* (Atlanta: Mockingbird Books, 1975); *Reflections on Life After Life* (Atlanta: Mockingbird Books, 1977).

8. Dr. Karlis Osis and Dr. Erlendur Haraldsson, *What They Saw . . . At the Hour of Death* (N.Y.: Avon Books, 1977) pp. 205-206.

9. K. Rahner, *op. cit.*, pp. 66-71.

10. On this point cf. Rahner, *op. cit.* pp. 72-73.

11. C.S. Lewis, *The Screwtape Letters* (London: Bles, 1966) p. 46.

Chapter Three

1. Gabriel Marcel, *Being and Having: An Existentialist Diary* (London: Collins, 1965) p. 158.

Chapter Four

1. Cf. B.M. Ahern, C.P., "The Concept of Union with Christ After Death in Early Christian Thought," in *Proceedings of the 16th Annual Convention of the Catholic Theological Society of America* (June 19-22, 1961) pp. 7-10.

2. Enoch 22:9-11, cited by Charles V. Pilcher, *The Hereafter in Jewish and Christian Thought* (London: SPCK, 1940) p. 82.

3. In some of the Targums or Chaldean paraphrases of the Hebrew Scriptures we find repeated use of the word "Gehenna" to refer to a punishment by fire. On this point cf. *A Critical History of the Doctrine of a Future Life,* by Wm. R. Alger (N.Y.: W.J. Widdleton, Publisher, 1871) p. 328.

4. C.S. Lewis, *The Last Battle,* Vol. VII, *Chronicles of Narnia* (N.Y.: Macmillan, 1970) p. 154.

Chapter Five

1. Charles Williams, *All Hallows' Eve* (Noonday Press; Farrar, Straus and Giroux, 1969) p. 133.

2. Elmer O'Brien, "The Scriptural Proof for the Existence of Purgatory from 2 Maccabees—12:43-45" in *Sciences Ecclesiastiques,* 2 (1949), p. 108.

3. Joachim Gnilka, *1st 1 Kor. 3,10-15 ein Schriftzeugnis fur das Fegfeurer?* (Dusseldorf: M. Triltsch, 1955) pp.63-93.

4. St. Gregory of Nyssa, *Oratio de mortuis, PG* XLVI, 524 C-D.

5. Cf. F. Cayre, *Manual of Patrology* (Tournai: Desclee & Co., 1936) Vol. 1, p. 712.

6. B. Bartmann, *Purgatory* (London: Burns, Oates & Washbourne, Ltd., 1936) pp. 160-161.

7. Cf. R.J. Bastian, S.J., "Purgatory" in *New Catholic Encyclopedia* (N.Y.: McGraw-Hill Book Co., 1966) p. 1037.

8. K. Rahner, *On the Theology of Death*, p. 33.

9. K. Rahner, *Theological Investigations*, Vol. IV (Baltimore: Helicon Press, 1969) pp. 347-354.

10. Cf. R. Guardini, *The Last Things* (N.Y.: Pantheon, 1954) pp. 46-48.

11. Piet Fransen, S.J., "The Doctrine of Purgatory," in *Eastern Churches Quarterly*, no. 13, 1959 (p. 106).

12. Tertullian, *De corona mil.*, 3, *PL* II, 98-99.

13. Tertullian, *Monogamia*, 10, *PL* II, 992-993.

14. Council of Trent, Session 25, *DS.* 983.

15. Martin Jugie, A.A., *Purgatory and the Means to Avoid It;* tr. Malachy Gerard Carroll (Cork: The Mercier Press, 1949) p. 34.

16. Cf. K. Rahner, *On the Theology of Death*, pp. 27, 32-33; *Theological Investigations* Vol. 2, tr. Karl H. Kruger (London: Darton, Longman & Todd, 1963) pp. 197-198; *ibid.*, Vol. 3 (1967) p. 204.

17. K. Rahner, *Theological Investigations*, Vol. 2, p. 197.

18. M. Jugie, *op. cit.* pp. 49-50.

19. Cf. Robert Gleason, S.J., *The World to Come* (London: Sheed & Ward, 1959) pp. 100-102.

20. St. John of the Cross, *The Living Flame of Love*, Stanza 1, in *The Collected Works of St. John of the Cross*, tr. Kieran Kavanaugh, O.C.D.and Otilio Rodriguez, O.C.D. 1 CS Publications (Wash. D.C.: Institute of Carmelite Studies, 1973) p. 578.

21. *Ibid.*, p. 335.

22. St. Catherine of Genoa, *On Purgatory*, tr. Charlotte Balfour and Helen D. Irvine (N.Y.: Sheed & Ward, 1946) pp. 18-19.

23. St. Mark of Ephesus, *First Homily*, tr. Archimandrite Amvrossy Pogodin in *St. Mark of Ephesus and the Union of Florence* (Jordanville, N.Y.: Holy Trinity Monastery, 1963) p. 59.

24. Serge Bulgakov, *The Orthodox Church* (London: Centenary Press, 1935) pp. 208-209.

Chapter Six

1. F.X. Durrwell, *The Resurrection*, tr. Rosemary Sheed (N.Y.: Sheed & Ward, 1966) p. 210.

2. St. Clement, *First Epistle to the Corinthians*, V, 6 and VI, 1, *PG* I, pp. 217-220.

3. For detailed information cf. R.S. Bour, "La Communion des Saints attestee par les Monuments de l'Antiquite chretienne," in *Dictionaire de Theologie Catholique;* Vol. III, pp. 454-480.

4. Hippolytus, *Commentary on Daniel;* Band 1 ed. Bonwetsch; *Die Griechischen Christlichen Schriftsteller* (Leipzig: J.C. Hinrichs' sche, 1897) p. 28.

5. Origen, *On Prayer*, XI, 2 and XI, 1, *PG* XI, pp. 448-449.

6. St. Augustine, *Enchiridion*, 56, *PL* XL, p. 258 ff.

7. *Ibid.*, *De Civitate Dei*, X, 25, *PL* XLI, p. 303.

8. *Ibid.*, *Enarr. in Ps. XLIV*, 20, *PL* XXXVI, p. 507.

9. St. Basil, *Adversus Eunomium*, III, 1, *PG* XXXIX, 656 ff.; *De Spiritu Sancto*, 13, *PG* XXXIII, 120; St. Gregory of Nyssa, *De Vita Moisis*, *PG* XLIV, 337 ff.; St. John Chrysostom, *In Matt. homilia*, LIX, 4, *PG* LVIII, p. 579.

10. St. Basil, *Hom. in Ps.* XXXIII, 5, *PG* XXIX, p. 364.

11. *Ibid.*, *De Spiritu Sancto*, 13, *PG* XXXIII, p. 120; St. John Chrysostom, *In Epistle ad Coloss. 1, homilia III*, 4, *PG* LXII, p. 322.

12. St. Hilary, *In Ps. CXXIX*, 7, *PL* IX, p. 722.

13. Billy Graham, *Angels: God's Secret Agents* (Garden City, N.Y.: Doubleday & Co., Inc., 1975) pp. 148-149.

14. *Lumen Gentium*, No. 50.

15. St. John of the Cross, *The Spiritual Canticle*, p. 441.

16. Cited by John A.T. Robinson in his work, *In the End, God . . .* (London: J. Clarke 1950) p. 123.

17. Milton, *Paradise Lost*, IV, 677-678, in *Poetical Works* (Oxford: Clarendon Press, 1952-1955).

18. Translation given by Valentin-M. Breton, O.F.M., *The Communion of Saints* (London: Sands & Co., 1934) tr. by R.E. Scantlebury, p. 69.

Chapter Seven

1. G. Philips, "Reflections on Purely Conceptual and on *Real* Theology" in *Louvain Studies*, 26 (1969) p. 264.

2. Tertullian, *De Spectaculis*, Cap. XXX, *PL* I ,735-736.

3. St. Augustine, *De Civitate Dei*, Lib. XXI, Cap. 2-4, *PL* XLI, 709-712.

4. St. Thomas Aquinas, *Summa*, pars 3, Suppl. Quaest. 93, art. 1.

5. Jonathan Edwards, *Works* (N.Y. Burt Franklin, 1968) Vol. VIII, p. 166.

6. Ladislaus Boros, *We Are Future* (Garden City, N.Y.: Doubleday, 1973) p. 155.

7. C.S. Lewis, *The Great Divorce* (N.Y.: Macmillan, 1971) p. 18.

8. J.L. McKenzie, *Dictionary of the Bible* (Milwaukee: Bruce, 1965) pp. 300; 801.

9. Cf. J.T. Addison, *Life Beyond Death* (N.Y.: Houghton Mifflin Co., 1932) p. 215.

10. McKenzie, *op. cit.*, p. 300.

11. K. Rahner, "Hell" in *Sacramentum Mundi* (N.Y.: Herder & Herder, 1969) pp. 7-8.

12. B. Lonergan, *Method in Theology* (N.Y.: Herder & Herder, 1972) pp. 320, 325.

13. K. Rahner, *op. cit.*, p. 7. *DS* in this quotation stands for a collection of church documents well known to Catholic students of theology and refers to Denzinger-Schonmetzer: *Enchiridion Symbolorum, Definitionum et Declarationum* (Freiburg i. B. Herder, 1963).

14. It is not altogether clear that this was Origen's teaching. There are many texts of his that show he insists on the damned not being given another chance but will be sentenced to eternal punishment. Cf. G. Maloney, *Man — The Divine Icon* (Pecos, N.M.: Dove Publications, 1973) pp. 85-86.

15. Cf. *DS* 858; *DS* 1306; *DS* 801; *DS* 76; *DS* 1539, 1543, 1575, *DS* 1705.

16. Rev. Arthur Chambers, *Our Life After Death* (London: Charles Taylor, 1901) p. 141.

17. C.R. Smith writes that "extinction is not a biblical concept." Cf. *The Bible Doctrine of the Hereafter* (London: Epworth Press, 1958) p. 220.

18. K. Rahner, "The Hermeneutics of Eschatological Assertions," in *Theological Investigations*, Vol. IV (Baltimore: Helicon, 1966). On this subject see also E. Schillebeeckx, "The Interpretation of Eschatology," in

The Problem of Eschatology; Concilium, Vol. 41 (N.Y.: Paulist Press, 1969) pp. 42-56; Gregory Baum, *Man Becoming* (N.Y.: Herder, 1970) Ch. IV.

19. Cf. G. Baum, "Eschatology," in *Chicago Studies* (Fall, 1973) p. 309.

20. Patrick Fannon, "And After Death," in *Catholic Mind* (April, 1975) pp. 12-25.

21. C.S. Lewis, *The Great Divorce,* p. 128.

22. Emil Brunner, *The Divine-Human Encounter,* cited by John A.T. Robinson; *In the End, God.* . . (N.Y.: Harper & Row, 1968) p. 115.

23. Cited by Robinson, *op. cit.,* p. 123.

24. Robinson, *op. cit.,* pp. 122-123.

25. Albert Camus, *The Fall* (N.Y.: Vintage Books: Random House, 1956) tr. by Justin O'Brien, p. 118.

26. Hans Lietzmann, *A History of the Early Church* (N.Y.: Scribner's, 1961) Vol. 2, p. 310.

27. K. Rahner, "Hell," *op. cit.,* p. 8.

28. A. Winklhofer, *The Coming of His Kingdom* (N.Y.: Herder & Herder, 1963) pp. 96-97.

29. H. Urs von Balthasar, *Le chretien Bernanos* (Paris: Seuil, 1963) pp. 160-161.

30. Cf. H. Vorgrimler, "Christ's Descent into Hell: Is It Important?" in *Concilium,* 1, no. 2, (1966) pp. 75-81.

Chapter Eight

1. Cf. Walter Sullivan, "Experts Speculate about Possible Life in Other Worlds," in the *New York Times* (June 26, 1979) p. C3.

2. Bernard J. Boelen, *Personal Maturity* (New York: Seabury Press, 1978) p. 135.

3. Cf. S. Bulgakov, "De Verbe Incarne," in *La Sagesse Divine et la Theanthropie* (Paris: Aubier, 1943) pp. 65-68.

4. Cf. John L. McKenzie, S.J., *Dictionary of the Bible* (Milwaukee: Bruce Publishing Co., 1975) pp. 344-345 and J. Plastaras, "Heaven (In the Bible)," in *New Catholic Encyclopedia* (N.Y.: McGraw-Hill, 1966) Vol. 6, p. 968.

5. Cf. Mt. 25:34; 22:2; 25:10; Rv 21:9; Lk 14:16; Col 1:12; 1 Pt 1:4; Heb 11:16; 12:22; Rv 21:2-3; Heb 4:9; Rv 14:13.

6. St. Augustine, *In Psalmo* XLIX, no. 2, *PL* XXXVI, pp. 565-566.

7. St. Gregory of Nyssa, *On Perfection,* tr. by V. W. Callahan in *Ascetical Works: Fathers of the Church* (Wash. D.C., 1967) Vol. 58: p. 122.

8. St. Gregory of Nyssa, *Life of Moses* in *From Glory to Glory*, tr. and ed. by J. Danielou and H. Musurillo (N.Y.: 1961) p. 144.

9. St. Gregory of Nyssa, *Canticle of Canticles, op. cit.*, p. 270.

10. *Ibid.*

11. St. Gregory of Nyssa, *Life of Moses, op. cit.*, p. 144.

12. Piet Schoonenberg, S.J., "I Believe in Eternal Life," in *Concilium: Dogma, the Problem of Eschatology* (N.Y.: Paulist Press, 1969) p. 110.

13. Cf. G. Maloney, S.J., *A Theology of Uncreated Energies* (Milwaukee: Marquette Univ. Press, 1978).

14. St. Basil, *Epistle to Amphilochius*, cited by George Habra in "The Patristic Sources of the Doctrine of Gregory Palamas on the Divine Energies," in *Eastern Churches Quarterly*, 12 (1957-1958) p. 300.

15. Cf. *DS* 1000-1001; *DS* 1305.

16. K. Rahner, *Theological Investigations* (Baltimore: Helicon Press, 1964), Vol. 11, p. 215.

17. "The Pathway" was written in 1949 for the centenary commemoration of Bavarian composer Conradin Kreutzer's death.

Chapter Nine

1. Joachim Gnilka, "Contemporary Exegetical Understanding of 'The Resurrection of the Body,' " in *Immortality and Resurrection*, Vol. 60 of *Concilium* (N.Y. Herder & Herder, 1970) p. 129.

2. For further development on this theme, cf. J. McKenzie, *The Power and the Wisdom* (Milwaukee: Bruce Publ. Co., 1965) p. 114 ff.; Piet Schoonenberg, "He Emptied Himself" (Phil 2:7) in *Concilium*, no. 11 (N.Y. Paulist, 1965) pp. 47-66.

3. John Macquarrie: *Principles of Christian Theology* (N.Y., Scribner's, 1977) p. 316.

4. On this point, cf. F.X. Durrwell, C.SS.R., *The Resurrection*, tr. Rosemary Sheed (N.Y. Sheed & Ward, 1966) pp. 1-34.

5. E. Kasemann, "The Pauline Theology of the Cross," which appeared in the journal, *Interpretation;* Vol. XXIV, no. 2, p. 177, cited by Lloyd Geering, *Resurrection: A Symbol of Hope* (London: Hodder & Stoughton, 1971) p. 225.

6. Jurgen Moltmann, *Theology of Hope* (N.Y.: Harper & Row, 1967) pp. 76-84; 172-182, 302.

7. Cf. P.C. Hodgson, *Jesus-Word and Presence* (Philadelphia: Fortress Press, 1971) pp. 220-291.

8. Representative of this school is Lloyd Geering, *Resurrection: A Symbol of Hope* (London: Hodder & Stoughton, 1971) pp. 216-233.

9. This was the theme that I developed in *Invaded by God: Mysticism and the Indwelling Trinity* (Denville, N.J.: Dimension Books, 1979).

10. Joseph Huby, *Les Epitres de la Captivite* (Paris: Beauchesne, 1935) p. 40, cited by Christopher Mooney, S.J., "The Body of Christ in the Writings of Teilhard de Chardin" in *Theological Studies*, 25 (Dec. 1964) pp. 604-605.

11. Cf. *DS* 11; 30; 76; 150; 801; 859.

12. Maurice Carrez, "With What Body Do the Dead Rise Again?" in *Immortality and Resurrection, op. cit.*, p. 93.

13. Pierre Benoit, O.P., "Resurrection: At the End of Time or Immediately After Death?" in *Immortality and Resurrection, op. cit.*, pp. 103-114.

14. *Ibid.*, p.109.

15. *Acta Apostolicae Sedis (AAS)* 42 (1950), p. 770.

16. Donal Flanagan, "Eschatology and the Assumption" in *The Problem of Eschatology: Concilium;* Vol. 41 (N.Y.: Paulist Press, 1969) pp. 140-146.

17. Joseph Bonsirven, S.J., *Theology of the New Testament* (Westminster, Md.: Newman Press, 1962) p. 148.

18. Typical of such popular visions of heaven and the life to come that put the emphasis on what man is going to get out of heaven are: Anne Sandberg, *Seeing the Invisible* (Plainfield, N.J.: Logos International, 1977); Elizabeth Bossert, *My Visit to Heaven* (Jacksonville, Florida: Higley, 1968): Gordon Lindsay, *Paradise, Abode of the Righteous Dead* (Dallas: The Voice of Healing, 1967); Hal Lindsey, *There's a New World Coming* (Santa Ana: Vision House, 1973); Karl Sabiers, *Where Are the Dead?* (Los Angeles: Christian Pocket Books, 1959; Anne Terry White, *All About the Stars* (N.Y.: Random House, 1954).

19. J.B.S. Haldane, *Possible Worlds and Other Essays*, p. 210 cited by L. Geering, *op. cit.* p. 210.

20. Jurgen Moltmann, *Theology of Hope* (N.Y.: Harper & Row, 1968) p. 338.

Appendix One

1. St. Augustine, *De Peccatorum Meritis*, I, XXI; *PL* XLIV, p. 120.

2. *DS* 780.

3. *DS* 858; 1306.

4. *DS* 1512; 1513; 1524.

5. George Dyer, *Limbo, Unsettled Question* (N.Y.: Sheed & Ward, 1964); Cf. also his article, "Limbo, a Theological Evaluation," in *Theological Studies,* 19 (1958) pp. 32-49 and "The Unbaptized Infant in Eternity," in *Chicago Studies,* 2 (1963) pp. 141-153. See also William A. Van Roo, S.J., "Infants Dying Without Baptism: A Survey of Recent Literature and Determination of the State of the Question," in *Gregorianum,* 35 (1954) pp. 406-473 and Peter Gumpel, S.J., "Unbaptized Infants: May They Be Saved?" in *Downside Review,* 72 (1954) pp. 342-458; *Ibid.* 73 (1955) pp. 317-346.

6. M. Laurenge, "Esquisse d'une etude sur le sort des enfants morts sans bapteme," in *L'Annee Theologique Augustinienne;* Vol. XIII (1952).

7. V. Wilkins, S.J., *From Limbo to Heaven* (N.Y.: Sheed & Ward, 1961).

8. P. Glorieux, "Endurcissement final et graces dernieres," in *Nouvelle Revue Theologique,* Vol. LIX (1932); L. Boros, *The Mystery of Death* (N.Y.: Herder & Herder, 1965).

Appendix Two

1. Dr. Raymond Moody, *Life After Life* (Atlanta, Ga.: Mockingbird Books, 1975). A sequel to this is his *Reflections on Life After Life* (N.Y.: Bantam-Mockingbird, 1977).

2. Dr. E. Kubler-Ross *On Death and Dying* (N.Y.: Macmillan Co., 1971) and *Death: The Final Stage of Growth* (N.J.: Prentice-Hall, Inc., 1975).

3. W.Y. Evans-Wentz, ed., *The Tibetan Book of the Dead* (N.Y.: Oxford Univ. Press, 1960).

4. Cf. E.A. Poe, "A Descent into the Maelstrom," in *The Complete Tales and Poems of Edgar Allen Poe* (N.Y.: Modern Library, 1938).

5. Dr. K. Osis and Dr. E. Haraldsson, *Deathbed Observations by Physicians and Nurses: A Cross-cultural Survey* (N.Y.: Parapsychology Foundations, 1962); and *At the Hour of Death* (N.Y.: Avon, 1977).

6. Cited in an article by Dr. Michael B. Sabom and Sarah A. Kreutziger, "Physicians Evaluate the Near Death Experience," in *The Journal of the Academy of Religion and Psychical Research;* Vol. 2, no. 2 (April, 1979) p. 72.

7. Dr. Robert Crookall, *The Supreme Adventure* (London, James Clarke, 1961); *The Study and Practice of Astral Projection* (London: Aquarian Press, 1961); *More Astral Projections* (London: Aquarian Press, 1964); *Case-Book of Astral Projection* (Secaucus, N.J.: University Books, 1972).

8. The most famous living OBE "trancer" is an ordinary businessman in Virginia, Robert Monroe, who in his work, *Journeys Out of the Body* (N.Y.: Doubleday and Co., 1971), describes simple techniques that have allowed him to enter into an OBE through a self-induced trance. Other works, besides those written by R. Crookall, include: S.J. Muldoon and H. Carrington, *The Projection of the Astral Body* (London: Rider & Co., 1929); Susy Smith, *The Enigma of Out-Of-Body Travel* (N.Y.: Helix Press, 1965).

9. We have seen many references in the course of this book to such a view of the total person dying and the total person possessing a new cosmic relationship of spiritualized body-soul-spirit relationships to the world around him. Cf. chapter one of this work.

10. Dr. Malachi B. Martin, "Life After Death" as reprinted in *The Journal of the Academy of Religion and Psychical Research*, pp. 50-51. This originally appeared in the March 18, 1978 issue of *National Review.*

11. D. Scott Rogo, "Research on Deathbed Experiences: Some Contemporary and Historical Perspectives," in *The Journal of the Academy of Religion and Psychical Research*, p. 47.

12. Dr. John Palmer, "The Out of Body Experience: A Psychological Theory," in *The Journal of the Academy of Religion and Psychical Research*, pp. 52-57. Other psychologists propose a similar theory, such as J. Ehrenwald, "Out-of-the-Body Experience and the Denial of Death," in *Journal of Nervous and Mental Diseases*, no. 159 (1974) pp. 227-233; M. Grosso, "Some Varieties of Out-of-Body Experience," *Journal of the American Society for Psychical Research*, no. 70 (1976) pp. 179-193; R. Noyes, "The Experience of Dying," in *Psychiatry*, no. 35 (1972) pp. 174-184, and C.T. Tart, "A Psychophysical Study of Out-of-the-Body Experiences in a Selected Subject," in *Journal of the American Society for Psychical Research*, no. 62 (1968) pp. 3-27.

13. John Palmer, *op. cit.*, p. 55.